GREATEST
MOMENTS
C A N A  D I A N
HOCKEY

J. Alexander Poulton

OVER
TIME
BOOKS

© 2005 by OverTime Books
First printed in 2005 10 9 8 7 6 5 4 3 2 1
Printed in Canada

The Publisher: OverTime Books is an imprint of Éditions de
                      la Montagne Verte

Library and Archives Canada Cataloguing in Publication

Poulton, J. Alexander (Jay Alexander), 1977–
   Greatest moments in Canadian hockey / J. Alexander Poulton.

Includes bibliographical references.

   ISBN-13: 978-0-9737681-4-1
   ISBN-10: 0-9737681-4-2

   1. Hockey—Canada—History. I. Title.

GV848.4.C3P69 2005   796.962'0971   C2005-905014-4

Project Director: J. Alexander Poulton
Project Editor: Tom Monto
Production: Jodene
Cover Design: Valentino
Cover Image: Team Canada's win at the 1972 Summit Series.
Courtesy of Getty Images / Melchior DiGiacomo (photographer)

PC: P5

Table of Contents

Dedication

To Papa

~❦~

Introduction

Countless moments in the history of the game of hockey are considered great. Those who watched the Summit Series in 1972 say that Henderson's goal qualifies as one of the greatest. A Montréaler during the '40s considers many of Maurice Richard's exploits great moments. Also, Wayne Gretzky's many records, goals, cups and awards can be considered as belonging among the greatest moments in hockey.

Looking through the greatest moments in hockey, it was difficult to choose those that stand out as the best. I have tried to choose a variety of moments to cover the range from the Montréal Canadiens winning the Stanley Cup five times in a row to the tough-as-nails defenceman Bob Baun playing the Cup finals on a broken leg. There are other moments that definitely had to be in the book, such as the Leafs winning the Cup in '67 and the Gretzky trade to the Los Angeles Kings.

In choosing the defining moments of hockey, I focused on professional leagues and the international tournaments that have become the measuring stick for the best hockey in the world. I wanted to present an even-handed view of the events that have marked hockey for better and worse.

All that remains of some moments are faded images of long-dead players—yet these stories are full of life and provide unique insight into a long-ago time still close to our hearts. To see the impact these stories have on fans, you just have to look at Maurice Richard. He moved the Canadiens' fans and many Quebecers like no other person in hockey history. At the closing ceremony of the Montréal Forum when Maurice Richard came out on the ice, he received the loudest and longest standing ovation of his career. This was somewhat odd because most of the people in the arena were too young to have seen Richard play hockey. His legacy and the images that remained from his heyday moved those in attendance to cheer for 15 minutes and brought the old hockey player to tears.

Some of the famous moments in hockey history were made by players who never received the level of recognition of Gretzky or Richard. Each of their moments of glory put a mark on the history of hockey to such a degree that the mention of their names evokes memories of the moments they helped make happen. For instance, Bill Barilko was a defenceman who could be relied on to cover his man and hold his position, but he is remembered as the player who scored the game-winning goal against the Montréal Canadiens in the 1951 Stanley Cup Finals. He unfortunately is also remembered for his tragic death when the plane he was in crashed in a place so remote that the wreckage was not found until 10 years later.

Then there are players who made names for themselves by breaking social barriers. They are remembered as the first ones to cross the "lines." Willie O'Ree has the distinction of being the first black player to play in the National Hockey League. Although his on-ice work in the league was less than remarkable, he opened the world of hockey to a new group of young players who had thought hockey was off-limits to them.

Some great hockey moments are not based on glory. Tragic moments mark the history of hockey as much as winning moments do. When Howie Morenz died in 1937, the hockey world lost its first superstar and its ambassador for the game in the U.S. In the time before Gretzky's move to Los Angeles, Morenz popularized hockey in the United States, where earlier the country had no more than faint interest in the sport. The U.S.A. was a baseball nation at the time, but when the Canadiens played in the U.S., Americans turned out by the thousands to see the "Stratford Streak" play.

The Richard Riot of 1955, although a sad moment for hockey, was a defining moment in the life and career of Maurice Richard and for the history of the Montréal Canadiens. The story of how a small incident on the ice between Richard and Boston's Hal Laycoe turned into a full-scale riot that caused damages of $100,000 for the city of Montréal has been attached to the Rocket's legacy and is a part of the history of the NHL.

Good or bad, these moments are the moments that hockey fans dream of and hockey players aspire to be involved in.

A photo of Wayne Gretzky expresses the passion perfectly. Gretzky first won the Stanley Cup in 1984. The photo was taken the moment before he was handed the Cup and shows a look on his face of such joy and excitement that you can tell he had been dreaming of that moment all his life.

It is moments like this that we remember, and it is these moments that keep us going back for more. Game on!

Greatest Moments in Canadian Hockey includes moments that do not appear to be strictly Canadian. But you will find that Canadian hands somehow touched every moment herein. The 1980 U.S. Olympic team's "Miracle on Ice" was included because Canadians appreciate stories about underdogs becoming champions, a story lived out in the 1972 Summit series against Russia. When the New York Rangers won the Stanley Cup in 1994, team captain Mark Messier, a Canadian, was the first Ranger to touch the Stanley Cup since they last won the trophy 54 years earlier. Wayne Gretzky, Bobby Orr and Lester Patrick all played and won for American teams, but they are all united by their Canadian origins. A Canadian game it was born, and a Canadian game it shall remain.

And the NHL Was Born...

When the National Hockey League formed in 1917, it seemed to be just another of the many hockey leagues that sprang up—and just as quickly failed—in Canada and the United States in the first few humble years of professional hockey. The league was not taken seriously; most people were focused on the war raging in Europe, and there was a shortage of able-bodied men to play the game.

With the folding of the National Hockey Association, the National Hockey League, led by its president Frank Calder, was formally established on November 26, 1917. It began the season with four teams. When the arena used by the Montréal Wanderers burned down, the team could not afford to rebuild and folded, becoming a footnote in hockey history. The three remaining teams—the Montréal Canadiens, the Toronto Arenas and the Ottawa

Senators—finished the season with Toronto coming out on top as the first Stanley Cup champions of the National Hockey League.

Despite the loss of the Wanderers and the lack of able-bodied men, the NHL firmly established itself as the premiere professional hockey league in North America. Fans flocked to games to see stars like the Canadiens' "Phantom" Joe Malone who scored 44 goals in just 20 games. Another star of the time was Senators' goaltender Clint Benedict who made saves by "accidentally" falling down so frequently that the league changed the rules so that goaltenders would not be given penalties for stopping the puck that way.

Through the years, the rules of the NHL have changed to meet the needs of fans and players. But the passion for the game remains as high as it was when the first puck was dropped at the first NHL game on December 19, 1917.

Chapter One

Greatest Team Moments

The Dawson City Challenge: The Great Northern Hope

In 1904, the Stanley Cup was barely 12 years old, but it had already become the defining treasure for any team out to prove they were the best in the world. That year, a group of ragtag adventurers from Dawson City, Yukon made history by challenging the Ottawa Silver Seven Hockey Club for the Cup.

Dawson City in 1904 was filled with many eccentric characters who had made their way north in search of fortunes during the Gold Rush. One larger-than-life character, Joseph Whiteside Boyle, decided to gather a team together under the name "Dawson City Nuggets" to travel south and challenge the Ottawa Silver Seven to a Cup showdown.

Ottawa accepted the challenge, and the northern-ers began to prepare a team to do battle with them.

Ottawa was not an easy team for the inexperi-enced Dawson City Nuggets to beat. The team was led by the infamous Frank "One-Eyed" McGee, a prodigious goal scorer who even to this day holds amazing records in Stanley Cup history. McGee was called "One-Eyed" because he had lost one of his eyes during a hockey game. The Silver Seven had four other players who were good enough to later be named to the Hockey Hall of Fame.

Dawson City pinned their hopes on 19-year-old goaltender Albert Forest, forwards Norman Watt, Dr. Randy McLennan, Hector Smith and George Kennedy, and defencemen Jimmy Johnstone and Archie Martin. Finally, Boyle had his team ready. The next problem was getting the team to Ottawa.

On December 18, 1904, the men from Dawson City started the long journey to Ottawa Some of the players began the journey on their bicycles, while others opted for a traditional means of trans-portation—hauling their bags on a dogsled. A sud-den thaw forced these players to walk. The team then took a train to Skagway, Alaska where they hoped to connect find a boat destined for Seattle, but they missed the boat by two hours. The next boat arrived five days later and carried them to Seattle. The weary travellers then backtracked to Vancouver to catch a train east. Weather-beaten, tired and not too steady on their feet, the Dawson

City Nuggets arrived in Ottawa 25 days later. The news that a team from Dawson City, Yukon, had journeyed to Ottawa by foot, bike, sled, boat and train spread through the local papers. Just two days later, they played their first game.

Unprepared, Dawson City was easily defeated 9–3. However, to the credit of the Nuggets, they held "One-Eyed" McGee to only 1 goal. Unfortunately, this was the only good thing to come out of the two-game series for the players from Dawson City. The next game they suffered the worst loss in Stanley Cup history. Led by the amazing Frank "One-Eyed" McGee, the Ottawa Silver Seven scored 23 goals to the Dawson City Nuggets' 2. McGee scored an amazing 14 goals; 8 of which were scored in less than nine minutes; 4 were put in the back of the net in 140 seconds; and the sixth, seventh and eighth goals were scored in less than 90 seconds.

Making their way back to the Yukon, the Dawson City Nuggets enjoyed the fame that had followed them from Dawson City, playing teams in Kingston and Winnipeg. Just outside Whitehorse, where a celebration awaited them, a few of the players walked the remaining distance to receive the applause from fans along the road.

After the excitement from the Stanley Cup showdown died down, Boyle, always searching for adventure, financed his own machine-gun military unit in World War I, and later, during the Russian

Revolution, was active in Russia and Romania where he tried to rescue the Royal families. Apparently, in those days, a dynamic character like Boyle was needed to lead a group of men across Canada to play hockey.

After that 2-game series, the trustees of the Stanley Cup changed the rules so that only established teams with a "right" to challenge were allowed to play for the Cup. Never again would an unproven hockey team have the chance to fight for the right to hoist the Stanley Cup above their heads. Joe Boyle and his Nuggets did not take the Cup north to Dawson City, but they did create an interesting chapter in the quest for the Stanley Cup.

The Birth of Two Dynasties: The Montréal Canadiens and the Toronto Maple Leafs

No other sport has been marked by the legacy of two teams like the Montréal Canadiens and the Toronto Maple Leafs. These teams have etched their names into the history of the NHL. Their wins, losses and rivalries shaped the history of the NHL and created a mystique around the teams that survives in the passions of their fans to this day.

The Montréal Canadiens began its life in 1909, prior to the founding of the National Hockey League, when an Irishman from Ontario founded a team in Montréal with the bleu, blanc, rouge (blue, white and red) colours later made famous by the NHL Montréal Canadiens.

Hockey had long been the domain of the Anglophone upper crust in Montréal with teams like the Montréal Shamrocks and the Victorias. The Francophone majority had never had a team of its own. Shrewd businessman that he was, Ambrose O'Brien established an all-Francophone team that he expected would attract the large French population to games and would be more profitable than the English clubs that had come and gone.

When team manager Jack Laviolette announced the team would be named "Les Canadiens," the English-language newspaper in Montréal, *The Gazette*, exclaimed the new team would have trouble filling its ranks because "French-Canadian players of class are not numerous."

The Canadiens soon proved the naysayers wrong as it built one of the most successful sports franchises ever. The team has won 24 Stanley Cups and boasts many Hall of Famers, including Georges Vezina and Maurice Richard.

The existence of the Toronto Maple Leafs, oddly enough, is directly connected to the birth of the Montréal Canadiens. When the Canadiens were founded, there was already a hockey team with the name Canadiens in existence in a different league, the Club Athletique Canadien. In 1910, the owner of that team, George Kennedy, claimed the rights to the name Canadien and saw the name confusion as his opportunity to move to the professional ranks. The leaders of the National Hockey Association, fearing a hefty lawsuit, gave Kennedy the new Canadiens' franchise. Kennedy then sold the original Canadiens team to Toronto, where they took the name "Toronto Arenas."

In 1918, the Toronto Arenas won the first Stanley Cup in the newly formed National Hockey League. The team later changed its name to the "St-Patrick's" before adopting the moniker "Maple Leafs" in 1926 after Conn Smythe purchased the team. The Leafs won the Stanley Cup in 1932 and became one of the best teams in the NHL.

Hockey Night in Canada Goes on the Airwaves

On the night of October 11, 1952, at a game between the Montréal Canadiens and the Toronto Maple Leafs, Canadians in homes across the country got their first taste of what has become a Saturday night tradition with the first televised broadcast of the Canadian Broadcasting Corporation's (CBC) Hockey Night in Canada. A country that had been getting its hockey fixes over the radio from the voice of Foster Hewitt was able to watch its hockey heroes on the ice for the first time.

For more than 50 years, Hockey Night in Canada has stayed much the same, even in the current era of 30 NHL teams and playoff games in June and despite the disastrous experiment with the highlighted puck.

The Toronto Maple Leafs:
The Comeback of 1942

In 1941, it seemed that history has been against the Toronto Maple Leafs. Since the last time they had won the Stanley Cup in 1932, they had been in the finals six times in the previous nine years, and each time they could not seem to finish the job. Frustrated with their recurrent fate, Coach Dick Irvin resigned and handed the job over to former player Hap Day. This decision reversed the fortunes of the Leafs and put them near the top of the league.

Finishing the 1941–42 regular season in second place in the overall standings, the Leafs were in a good position at the start of the playoffs. However, as every hockey fan knows, the playoff series is a new season, and the best team in the regular season has often fallen in the first round of the playoffs. Coach Day took nothing for granted. The Maple Leafs had seen the Cup slip away before, and Day was determined to bring championship status to the city of Toronto that year.

History seemed destined to repeat itself. The Leafs' first playoff match was against the New York Rangers, the top team during the season and favourites to win the Cup. Even though the Rangers had the top two scorers in the NHL, they fell behind the Leafs three games to two. Toronto was poised to head into the Cup final. A dramatic goal by Maple Leafs forward Nick Metz with seven seconds remaining in the third period of game six gave the Leafs victory over the tough Rangers' squad. The 14,000 fans at Maple Leaf Gardens rose from their seats, chanting in unison, "Go, Leafs, Go!" as they began to have hope the team might win the Cup. If the Maple Leafs could beat the Rangers, the crowd had reason to expect Maple Leafs would beat their next opponent, the Detroit Red Wings, with ease and lift the Cup's curse.

Newspapers, fans and those in the hockey world all had the Maple Leafs as the odds-on favourite to win the Cup. The Leafs had finished 15 points ahead of the Wings at the end of the regular season and had triumphed over what was thought to be the best team in the League. Although the Red Wings had not been expected to run away with the series, it seemed judging by the first two games that the Leafs were about to repeat their old ways and lose the Stanley Cup finals again. Detroit had an answer for everything the Leafs threw at them. The pattern continued into the third game on April 9 in Detroit as the Leafs lost 5–2 and were only one loss away from losing the Cup.

After the third game, the feeling in the Leafs' dressing room was close to complete defeat. Goaltender Turk Broda knew that Detroit would not fold easily and that the Leafs were going to have trouble winning one game, let alone four in a row.

"Detroit is unbeatable. They can't seem to do anything wrong," said Broda after the third-game loss in Detroit.

Red Wings Coach Jack Adams had paid attention to the scouting reports on the Maple Leafs, and he adopted the system of icing the puck and simply out-hustling and out-working the Leafs in the corners. The Detroit newspapers had already wrapped the series up and were pontificating on who would win the MVP.

On the Maple Leafs' side of things, the outlook was not rosy. The Maple Leafs had not been able to overcome the Red Wings' defence, buttressed by the goaltending of Johnny Mowers, to get more than 2 goals in a game. Toronto sportswriters were merciless in their persecution of Coach Day, saying he wasn't prepared for Detroit and that the series was all but over. One Toronto Star reporter echoed the sentiment when he wrote, "Except for the gate receipts and the records, there is little apparent use in prolonging this series."

Hap Day wasn't one to give up easily. He knew he would have to do something drastic to keep the team from giving up on the goal they had worked towards all season, but he was at a loss to know what that drastic something should be. He had put all his star players on the ice, and they hadn't been able to break the Detroit system.

Day decided to bench scoring-ace Gord Drillion and lumbering defenceman Bucko McDonald in favour of benchwarmers Don Metz and Ernie Dickens who were more suited to the dump-and-chase style that the Red Wings had adopted.

In the dressing room prior to the start of game four, Day talked to his players. Pacing back and forth in the Leafs' dressing room with the Detroit crowd chanting in the background, Day waved a copy of the Detroit newspaper that sounded the death knell of his team. "The Detroit papers say we are finished. Hell, even the Toronto papers have written us off, but I ain't about to write us off," exclaimed Day loudly. Day read a letter from a 14-year-old Leafs' fan who still believed her favourite team could beat the Red Wings and win the Cup. The moment Day finished reading the letter, winger Billy Taylor yelled, "We'll win it for the little girl! We're not licked yet." This was the reaction Day had wanted from his team.

The Red Wings' celebrations were put on hold as the Maple Leafs won game four 4–3. At the end of the game, the Red Wings lost their coach. The coach tried to attack the referee in revenge for several questionable calls against his team and was suspended for the remainder of the series. The Leafs' fortunes seemed to be turning in their favour.

In game five, the Leafs easily won 9–3. They were led by replacement player Don Metz who scored a hat trick, thereby proving to skeptical Toronto sportswriters that Coach Day had done right in benching Gord Drillion. Game 6 saw Turk Broda redeem himself for the three losses at the start of the series by shutting out the Red Wings. As they went into game seven, Detroit team members scratched their heads, wondering what had happened to their three-game lead.

With the Toronto papers and fans back on the bandwagon, game seven at the Maple Leaf Gardens was the biggest show in town and drew a record 16,218 fans hoping to watch the Leafs' amazing comeback end in glory. By the end of the second period, the score was even with 1 goal apiece. The Leafs' owner, Conn Smythe, passionate about his team, entered the dressing room during the second intermission and gave a pep talk to his noticeably nervous players. His inspirational speech seemed to work on the Leafs as they took to the ice for the start of the third period accompanied by loud cheers from the fans filling the arena. The noise at the Gardens got louder when Red Wings goaltender Johnny Mowers left his net to stop an errant shot. The puck took an awkward bounce away from Mowers and ended up on the stick of Leafs forward Pete Langelle who simply tapped the puck into the empty Detroit net.

"The puck happened to bounce ten feet from Mowers, and I kinda banged at it," said Langelle after the game. "Next thing I knew, the red light was on, and we were ahead."

With a few minutes remaining, Dave Schriner potted the insurance goal as the Leafs won the greatest Stanley Cup comeback in NHL history.

The Greatest of All: The 1959–60 Montréal Canadiens

The victorious tradition of the Montréal Canadiens was established during the late 1950s when they were the best team in the NHL and probably the world. Hector "Toe" Blake had put together a team and a system that was difficult to beat, and the team was almost impossible to contain. A new religion developed under the lights of the Montréal Forum during the 1950s as people's hopes and dreams were invested in the exploits of the men who took to the ice in the jerseys of the Montréal Canadiens.

The Canadiens' dominance of the game during that decade changed the way the game is played. Great moments during those years of NHL dominance are too numerous to choose just a few. Aside from their five Stanley Cups victories in a row, they also broke records and changed the rules of the game.

After exorcising the demons of the "Richard Riots," the Canadiens came to the beginning of the 1955–56 season ready to reassert their position as the top team in the league. The previous spring's suspension of Richard, the subsequent riot and the team's loss to the Detroit Red Wings in the Stanley Cup final were memories the Canadiens wanted to put behind them at the start of the new season.

The Canadiens had the right ingredients for a great season: a brick-wall defensive core led by

Doug Harvey; one of the best goaltenders to play the game, Jacques Plante; and a full stable of goal scorers led by Captain Maurice Richard. However, a great team on paper does not always translate into a winning team. In those years, though, in addition to its talented individuals, the Montréal teams possessed a camaraderie that formed great individuals into a great team. With the keen coaching mind of Blake, the Canadiens became unstoppable.

Maurice "the Rocket" Richard was the heart of the team, both on and off the ice. On-ice, he was one of the most feared goal scorers and was well known for his tough antics—he could take control of a game single-handedly. Off the ice, Maurice Richard was elevated to the status of hero in Montréal and Québec. Without Maurice Richard, the Canadiens' dynasty might never have happened.

In the 1950s, the Canadiens brought home all the records and captured the imagination of hockey fans in Québec and across Canada. The 1959–60 season was the team's best.

"You can take any position. Jacques Plante in the nets and the defence group, led by the great Doug Harvey," recalled Jean Beliveau about the Canadiens' dominance during the roaring 1950s. "We had two good offensive lines plus a third line that was very good defensively. One night when one line had a problem, the other would pick up the slack."

The Montréal Canadiens' road to their fifth Stanley Cup was sweet. They finished the 1959–60 regular season at the top of the league in points, and three of their players were listed among the top 10 scorers in the league. There was little doubt across the NHL and among fans that the Canadiens would take the Stanley Cup to Montréal for a fifth straight time.

The first two games of the semi-finals against the Chicago Blackhawks were close, but both times Montréal won by 1 goal. In games three and four, Montréal's defensive core led by Doug Harvey and backed by the skilled goaltending of Jacques Plante shut down Bobby Hull and the Blackhawks 4–0 and 2–0. Although Chicago had star players, such as Hull and Stan Mikita, and the reliable goaltending of Glenn Hall, it could not match the Canadiens' depth. Blackhawks Coach Rudy Pilous put his checking lines out against Beliveau and Geoffrion, but then other players stepped in to score goals. Montréal easily won the series, four games to none and had a few days to wait for the outcome of the Toronto-Detroit series, which Toronto won with a 4–2 victory in game six.

Before the start of the finals against the Canadiens, Toronto Maple Leafs Coach Punch Imlach tried the psychological games for which he had become famous in previous playoffs. He claimed the Canadiens were so good that anything less than winning the Stanley Cup would be a huge defeat for them. This bit of reverse psychology had no effect on the hardened veterans, and the Canadiens easily took game one, scoring 3 goals before the 12-minute mark of the first period on their way to a 4–2 victory.

Game two had the same results as the Canadiens scored 2 quick goals, and Plante did the rest. The Canadiens scored a 2–1 victory and newspapers across the country predicted another Stanley Cup for Montréal. Game three proved an easy victory for the Canadiens with a score of 5–2. During that game, the Rocket scored his first goal of the 1960 playoffs and the 82nd in his career.

It turned out to be the last goal Richard would score for the Montréal Canadiens. Richard thought there was no better way to end his career than to have lifted the Stanley Cup over his head one more time, so that fall, before the start of the new season, he announced his retirement after 18 remarkable seasons with the Canadiens. His teammates were not surprised by the decision because Richard was plagued by injuries, had lost his flair for scoring and was tipping the scales at more than 90 kilograms.

The Canadiens went on to an easy victory in game four as Plante shut out the Leafs in a 4–0 win before a subdued crowd of 13,000 fans at Maple Leaf Gardens. Montréal had won its fifth straight championship, an accomplishment no other North American professional sports team had done to that date. After eight straight wins and five Stanley cups in a row, you might expect the Canadiens' victory celebrations to have been a raucous affair. But as Doug Harvey said to reporters after the game, "When you win eight straight games in the playoffs and you win five Cups in a row, there's not a whole lot to get excited about."

On December 3, 1960, Trent Frayne, a writer for the Maclean's magazine, wrote, "Nothing they have achieved in the dimming past compares with their monstrous domination of the game today. The questions naturally arise: How did they get that way? Is the end in sight?"

History answered that question, as the Canadiens did not make it to the Stanley Cup finals again until 1965. However, during the dry years of the early 1960s, the Canadiens built a base that allowed the team to dominate the League during the late 1960s, when they won the Stanley Cup another four times.

The '67 Leafs: The Last Hurrah

The 1966–67 Toronto Maple Leafs were a team of over-the-hill veterans and rookies still wet behind the ears. No one expected them to make it far into the playoffs. At the beginning of January 1967, Toronto writers had already written off the abilities of the team and its cantankerous coach, Punch Imlach. At one point during the season, Toronto lost 10 games in a row and blamed its losses on the lack of communication between players and coaches. Seeing the stress Imlach was under, the team physician ordered him to take time off. Replaced by Leafs' legend King Clancy, a weight seemed to lift off the team's shoulders. By the end of the season, the Leafs had secured third place and headed into the first round of the playoffs against the first-place Chicago Blackhawks.

Many of the veterans on the team expected the 1966–67 season to be their last. Several of the players were in their late 30s; others were in their early 40s. All had seen better days. The Toronto team felt only muted optimism as it dressed for game one of the Chicago series.

The game began evenly enough, but the Blackhawks' speed and the combined firepower of forwards Stan Mikita and Bobby Hull were too much for Toronto goalie Terry Sawchuk. By the end of the third period, the Blackhawks fans got what they had come for. Their team had taken game one 5–2. Chants of "Goodbye, Terry" filled the stadium as the Leafs left the ice.

Confident after their win, the Blackhawks took the next two days off. Not one for giving his players an easy time, Imlach put his team straight to work, and the effort paid off.

A strategy of battling hard in the corners and aggressively checking the star forwards worked to the Maple Leafs' advantage in game two. They defeated the Blackhawks 3–1. This time it was the Blackhawks' fans who quietly exited the building. Game three in Toronto was almost an exact repeat of the previous game as the "over-the-hill gang" outworked the baffled Blackhawks who could not overcome the lightning-fast reflexes of Terry Sawchuk.

Punch Imlach was proud of his team's efforts but made them work prior to game four. Imlach's strategy seemed to be, "I'll make them hate me so much that they will take out their anger on the Blackhawks."

The Hawks could not figure out how to break the tight-checking style of the Leafs, and although they won game four, the Blackhawks were outplayed on almost every level.

The Maple Leafs won the next two games, doing what no one had expected them to. The so-called "over-the-hill gang" had defeated the younger and more talented Chicago Blackhawks. Leafs defenceman Larry Hillman summarized their approach to the Chicago series, "We just worked at shutting down their stars. Everything revolved around their star players, Mikita and Hull. You shut them down; you shut the team down. With the Leafs, we had the team concept."

Meantime, the Montréal Canadiens were waiting patiently for the Stanley Cup final to begin. The Canadiens were good but not as good as earlier versions of the team that had dominated the game during the late 1950s. The Montréal team would dominate the league again during the 1970s after acquiring the goaltending skills of Ken Dryden. However, during the 1966–67 regular season, Montréal finished just two points ahead of the Maple Leafs.

The key for both teams in the 1967 finals was goaltending. Leafs goalies Sawchuk and Bower had proven themselves capable, but there were doubts that they could give consistent performances against the fast Montréal offence.

The Canadiens went with rookie goaltender Rogie Vachon, just 21, instead of veterans Gump Worsley and Charlie Hodge. Vachon had proven himself during the regular season, and Canadiens Coach Toe Blake felt the young goaltender could handle the pressure. Imlach immediately blasted Blake's prediction, ridiculing the goaltender's ability to play with the "big boys" in the Stanley Cup final.

"Tell that cocky Junior B goaltender that he won't be facing New York Rangers peashooters when the Leafs open up on him," said Imlach before the start of the series. "After we get through with Vachon, he may be back in Junior B."

Game one at the Forum did not turn out the way Imlach had planned. The Canadiens, coming off seven days of rest, easily handled the weary Leafs with a 6–2 victory before a capacity crowd at the Montréal Forum. The Leafs could not hold back the speedy Canadiens. They were forced to rely on their goaltender again and again, but Sawchuk did not have a good game. The Canadiens easily put the puck past the tired goaltender. Without great goaltending, a team does not get far in the NHL playoffs.

The Leafs were down but not out. Imlach assigned goaltender Johnny Bower to start game two at the Montréal Forum and give Sawchuk the rest he needed. At 42, Bower was not the popular choice for many to take on the Canadiens, but Imlach knew the veteran could handle the pressure. Bower did not disappoint.

That day, the Canadiens whipped 31 shots at Bower and not one found the back of the net. The Leafs, on the other hand, peppered Vachon with 43 shots, putting three of those into the net. Again as in the Chicago series, the Leafs had figured out a system to shut down their opponents. They aggressively checked the Canadiens' star players and pelted as many shots as possible at the rookie Canadiens goaltender. The strategy paid off as Bower and the Leafs shut out the Canadiens 3–0. The two teams headed to Toronto for game three.

The roar of the crowd the night of game three was almost deafening as Montréal and Toronto battled to a 2–2 tie by the end of the third period. As the game went into overtime, it seemed Bower and Vachon were ready to battle all night, and the other players knew the game would not end quickly or easily. A few close calls sent collective gasps through the crowd. One of the closest calls came when Yvan Cournoyer caught a pass from Jean Beliveau and cut his way through the defence. Cournoyer found only the goalie, Bower, left to stop him from scoring the winner. Cournoyer came in off the wing and tried to cut across the goal. Before Cournoyer could make Bower commit to the shot, Bower reached out with his stick and poked the puck away from the speeding Canadiens winger. After the game Bower noted his save as a critical moment:

> *I knew if I missed he would go right by me and have an open net for the game-winning goal, and I would look terribly foolish.*

A few minutes into the second overtime period, Toronto ended the game when Bob Pulford caught a goalmouth pass from Jim Pappin and shot the puck into the open Canadiens' net.

The Leafs lost game four with an embarrassing 6–2 loss, tying the series. But Toronto players and coaches still had faith they could beat the Canadiens and win the Stanley Cup.

With Johnny Bower out due to a groin pull, it was up to Terry Sawchuk to man the position between the pipes for the Leafs in game five. Sawchuk held the Canadiens to just 1 goal as Toronto scored a 4–1 victory. This victory gave them three games to the Canadiens' two.

"We had a good team in those years, really good," said Canadiens goaltender Gump Worsley after the series. "We should have won five straight. It was only one guy who beat us. One guy. Sawchuk."

Jean Beliveau echoed his statement:

We had no business losing in '67 to Toronto. Terry Sawchuk was the reason. I remember walking in on him all alone in a game in Toronto and how he stopped me. I still can't figure it out. I always had the feeling that if I score on that play, if he doesn't make that tremendous save, it very easily could have been another five Stanley Cups in a row.

It was May 2, 1967. The summer of love had begun, and the Leafs were poised to win the Stanley Cup. Before the start of the game, Punch Imlach, in one of his classic moments, dumped a large pile of money in the middle of the Leafs' dressing room, glared at the players and said, "This is what it's all about!" He then walked out of the room.

The first two periods of game six were exciting to watch as both teams fought hard to open scoring opportunities. Sawchuk proved to be the better goaltender that night, and the Leafs headed into the third period with a 2-goal lead. The Montréal Canadiens brought themselves within one goal of the Leafs with only a few minutes remaining in game time. The odds of a Canadiens' victory seemed bleak. With 55 seconds remaining, Blake pulled Worsley from the Montréal net in favour of the extra attacker. The face-off was set to the left of Sawchuk. Imlach put veterans Red Kelly, Tim Horton, Allan Stanley, Captain George Armstrong and Bob Pulford on the ice to play the remaining seconds, hoping they could hold back the Canadiens. With instructions to tie up the big Beliveau and prevent him from getting to the net, Stanley took the draw against the big Canadiens forward and held on to him for dear life until Red Kelly grabbed the loose puck and passed it to an open Pulford. Pulford, seeing Armstrong open on the right, shot him a quick backhand pass that landed exactly on the tape of his stick. With only Canadiens defenceman Jacques Laperriere back to defend the empty net Armstrong shot a quick wrist shot into the open net and secured the Leafs the Stanley Cup championship.

In front of capacity crowds at the Maple Leaf Gardens, the "over-the-hill gang" had taken the Cup away from two teams that most had predicted they could not beat.

With this game, the "Original Six" era came to an end. The next season saw the NHL expand south as teams in Minnesota, Philadelphia, Los Angeles and other U.S. cities added a new division to the league. Some said hockey would never be the same. In the Leafs' case, they were right. The 1967 Stanley Cup victory, the 11th in Toronto history, was their last.

"When they let me go for a youth movement in 1968," said defenceman Allan Stanley, "I often joked, 'They'll never win another Cup without me.' But geez, I didn't mean it."

Scotty Bowman Bows Out Gracefully

In a career filled with great moments, Scotty Bowman had his last when he hoisted the Stanley Cup above his head when his Detroit Red Wings won the Cup in 2002. It was the ninth cup of Bowman's career, putting him ahead of his idol Toe Blake as the coach with the most Stanley Cups. Bowman had 1244 career wins and an assured place in the Hockey Hall of Fame as one of the best coaches to stand behind a bench in the NHL.

Rangers End 54-Year Stanley Cup Drought

The world was not really focused on the start of the 1939–40 NHL season as World War II raged in Europe. The league chose to continue as usual, hoping they could remain financially viable. Fans worried that many of the established players would march off to war and that the league would be diluted with mediocre players. They worried the games would be boring to watch or ridiculously one-sided.

The 1939–40 New York Rangers had enough talent to ease the worries of the fans and even the skeptical sportswriters. Bryan Hextall, who was at the top of the NHL's list of scorers, and his linemates Phil Watson and Lynn Patrick led the team's powerful offence. In goal was Vezina Trophy winner Davey Kerr who was at the top of his game during the 1939–40 season and recorded a goals-against average of 1.54. The Rangers were set for a stellar season, and Coach Frank Boucher knew this was his chance to bring glory to the "Broadway Blueshirts."

During the season, the Rangers were a solid team that hovered near the top of the standings, and at one point won 14 straight home games. This season also saw another milestone in hockey with the first television broadcast of a NHL game. When the Rangers met the Montréal Canadiens at Madison Square Garden on February 25, 1940, the lens of one fixed-position camera scanned up and down the ice as the game was beamed into 300 television sets in the New York area. The quality of that television broadcasts was not what hockey fans enjoy today, but it was a start.

The Rangers went into the playoffs with qualified hopes of winning their third Stanley cup. The first round of the playoffs had the Rangers taking on the regular-season champion Boston Bruins in what promised to be a hard-fought series. The Rangers surprisingly disposed of the Bruins in six games and were set to face the Toronto Maple Leafs for the Stanley Cup. Although the Rangers finished several points ahead of the Maple Leafs during the regular season, no one on the Rangers' squad took victory over the Maple Leafs for granted. Toronto was a solid team backed by the solid goaltending of Turk Broda.

The Rangers won game one in overtime. The closeness of the game showed that the Rangers would have to work hard to win the Cup.

At the end of game four, the series between Toronto and New York was tied 2–2. Fans could only guess who would win the Cup. Nothing illustrated the deadlock better than game five in Toronto that went into two periods of overtime. The players sped up and down the ice trying to gain control of the game. Halfway through the second overtime, Rangers Coach Boucher put his best line on the ice, hoping to end the stalemate. Phil Watson got control of the puck and spotted Lynn Patrick moving in on the Bruin blue line. Watson floated a neat pass on to the stick of Patrick, who then blasted a shot past a noticeably tired Turk Broda. The Rangers' bench cleared, swarming Patrick in celebration. New York had the advantage they needed to secure the Stanley Cup.

Game six seemed a replay of game five as the two teams battled to a 2–2 tie at the end of third period. As the clock ran down in the third period, Watson thought he had ended the game when his shot beat Broda. However, the referee waved off the goal because another Rangers player had his skate in the crease. Fuming, Watson spat in the referee's face and would have attacked him if he had not been held back by his teammates. Miraculously Watson escaped without a penalty.

Again, the two teams went into sudden-death overtime, but this time it didn't take as long for a winner to be decided. At just 2:07 of the first overtime period, Watson shot a pass to Bryan Hextall who blasted the puck past Broda. As the Maple Leaf Gardens' crowd applauded politely, the Rangers' bench emptied onto the ice to celebrate their hard-earned 1940 Stanley Cup championship.

Following the on-ice celebrations, the Cup was carried to a Toronto hotel, where the players pouted beer and champagne into it. According to Brian Kendall in his book 100 Great Moments in Hockey, the Cup was reverently passed around, each player taking a sip from hockey's Holy Grail.

In the 1990s, fans of the other New York team, the Islanders, chanted "1940! 1940!" when the Rangers played in the Islanders' home arena, reminding the Rangers of the year they last had won the Stanley Cup. The Islanders had won four Stanley Cups during their 20-year history in the NHL, one more than the Rangers had achieved in the more than 60 years they had been in the league. Many called the Rangers' lack of success the result of a curse. To Rangers' fans, it seemed like a curse had to be responsible for the 54-years Stanley Cup drought.

Many hockey players and fans refer to the Stanley Cup as the Holy Grail of hockey. However, things that have happened to the Cup through the years besmirch its professed magical powers. Stories told of the Stanley Cup make players never want to drink out of it. One story has 1937 Detroit Red Wings' Gordon Pettinger using the Cup as a toilet during a drunken celebration. Another has Toronto Maple Leafs Red Kelly's son also mistaking the Cup for a toilet. When the toddler was placed in the Cup for a photograph, excitement got the better of the child and he befouled hockey's Holy Grail.

Still, despite its rough treatment, legend has it the Cup, like any sacred artifact, should not be defiled or desecrated lest harm or a curse will befall the defiler. Some say Rangers' president John Kilpatrick started a curse against the Rangers in 1940 when he burned the deed to the fully paid mortgage of Madison Square Garden in the bowl of the Cup. Rangers' fans and players had to wait a long time until their team won the Cup again.

In the early 1990s, the Rangers' curse seemed to be holding fast. The Rangers finished the 1992–93 season at the bottom of the league, failing again to make the playoffs.

However, the 1993–94 season was a complete turnaround for the beleaguered Rangers and their wallflower fans. Led by veteran captain Mark Messier, the Rangers surprised the league, finishing the season on top with 112 points and home-ice advantage going into the playoffs. Fate could not have written a better story when the Rangers eliminated the New York Islanders in four straight games and silenced the chants at the Nassau Coliseum. The Rangers then easily dispatched the Washington Capitals in five games in the conference semi-finals. The next two series proved more difficult and more rewarding.

The New Jersey Devils, their next opponent, had undergone a renaissance of their own under the tutelage of Coach Jacques Lemaire. The acrobatic goaltending of Martin Brodeur made the New Jersey team one of the best teams in the NHL in the 1990s. Lemaire had instituted a system of play known as the "trap" that focused on defence. By trapping the opponent offence in the neutral zone, the system makes it difficult for opponent's forwards to break over the blue line and overwhelm the goaltender as a unit. Rangers Coach Mike Keenan knew he had a challenge on his hands.

The Devils and Rangers played a nail-biting series. Games one and three went into double overtime with the teams sharing the victories evenly. By the end of game five, the Devils had a 3–2 lead in the series. The Rangers' curse seemed to be rearing its ugly head.

"It wasn't like you could avoid it," said Rangers Nick Kypreos. "It was everywhere—in the newspapers, on TV, from fans. You'd be getting to the arena two hours before a game, and 20 or 30 people would be at the gate to remind you."

They needed a miracle, and they got one from their captain. Before the start of game six, Messier predicted, "We know we're going to go in and win game six and bring it back for game seven."

Messier wasted no time in making his predictions come true. He led the way in game six with three goals, beating the Devils 4–2, tying the series and sending the teams into a pivotal game seven. Game seven was decided in double overtime. The Rangers then met the Vancouver Canucks in the Stanley Cup final.

The Rangers quickly established a 3–1 series lead over the Canucks but squandered their chance to end the series quickly as Vancouver clawed its way back to tie the series and send it to game seven in New York.

Madison Square Garden was abuzz with activity before the beginning of the game. The Cup was being polished in the back room as the players dressed for the game. This was the Rangers' chance to break the curse and bring the Cup back to Broadway. The pressure was on.

The capacity crowd at Madison Square Garden was well rewarded when the Rangers potted two goals in the first period and seemed to have a lock on the pace of the game. The game seemed to be finished once Messier scored to put the Rangers ahead 3–0 but the curse did not seem to be giving up easily. The Canucks clawed their way back with two goals by forward Trevor Linden. Rangers fans could feel the Cup slipping away as the seconds lingered on the clock. The game could not end fast enough for them. Rangers goaltender Mike Richter worked up a sweat as Canucks forwards peppered him with shot after shot. The last 60 seconds of the game saw the Canucks' goal empty, while the Canuck offence frantically tried to score. The crowd counted down the last seconds. The game was over.

Fans and players felt the weight of 54 years of disappointment lift as the Rangers finally became Stanley Cup champions again. As the Rangers players paraded the Cup around the arena, one long-time Rangers fan lifted a sign in the air that said, "Now I Can Die In Peace!"

Chapter Two

Greatest Individual Moments

Lester Patrick Plays in Net

In a scene out of a Hollywood movie, 44-year-old New York Rangers coach and manager Lester Patrick put on a pair of goalie pads and led his team to victory in the Stanley Cup playoff finals, securing a place in Hall of Fame history.

It happened in the 1928 Stanley Cup playoff finals when Lester Patrick's New York Rangers were taking on the Montréal Maroons in game two of a best-of-five series. The regular Rangers goaltender, Lorne Chabot, was taken out of the game with an eye injury. In the early days of hockey, teams did not have extra goaltenders as they do today. In those days, if a goaltender was injured, an emergency stand-in had to be used and had to be found quickly, or the team forfeited the game.

Patrick asked the Maroons' bench if Chabot could be replaced by the Ottawa Senators' outstanding goaltender, Alex Connell, who happened to be at the game that night. The Maroons quickly turned down that proposal and suggested a solution of their own.

"Why not put Lester in the net if you need a goaltender that bad?"

Patrick responded, "I will, by God. I will!"

Patrick had donned goalie pads on a few occasions but never in a high-pressure situation like the Stanley Cup finals. Quickly dressing himself in Chabot's gear, Patrick hit the ice, stretched his legs and readied himself for an attack.

He performed remarkably well. The Maroons peppered the grey-haired goaltender with shot after shot, but Patrick held firm. Crouching low to the ice, he was able to stop all but one shot that beat him in the third period, tying the game and sending it into overtime. During overtime, the stand-in goalie defended his goal successfully. The Rangers finally won the game with a goal by Frank Boucher. Patrick was hoisted atop his player's shoulders and paraded around the arena like a conquering hero.

After the game Patrick remarked on his performance, "I stopped only six or seven really hard shots. My teammates saved the old man with their back checking."

Patrick's stint in goal inspired the Rangers. Using a professional goaltender during the remainder of the series, the Rangers defeated the Montréal Maroons and brought the Stanley Cup to the United States for the second time in its history.

The Rocket's 50-in-50

Although his record has been broken since Maurice "the Rocket" Richard scored 50 goals in 50 games in 1944–45, history books talk about the first time that the achievement once thought impossible was reached.

Montréal Canadiens' scoring ace "Phantom" Joe Malone previously held the single-season record, with an amazing 44 goals in the 20-game 1917–18 season. As amazing as Malone's feat was, the hockey played in the first few years of the NHL was different than that played in the Rocket's time. The early rules favoured open-style games where offensive talents like Malone could flourish. Scoring 50 goals in a 50-game season became a goal for scoring aces to break. None have done it with more style than a young 23-year-old Montréal Canadiens forward named Maurice Richard.

By mid-season 1944–45, teamed with Elmer Lach and Toe Blake on what was aptly nicknamed the "Punch Line," Richard managed 29 goals in 27 games. Attention turned to the fiery young forward, and people began to believe that Richard would achieve the 50-goal mark. Richard also wanted the record in order to solidify his reputation as a goal-scoring forward who would not be pushed around. Earlier in his career, critics had stated doubts about his future, but they were silenced by his performance that season.

Richard once even carried a player on his back and scored a goal. "Over the years, people have asked me whether it was true that I actually scored a goal while carrying an opponent on my back, and the answer is 'yes,'" remarked Richard.

The amazing goal happened when the Canadiens were playing the Detroit Red Wings. As Richard broke free into the neutral zone, he had only to get past big Red Wings defenceman Earl Siebert to have a clear path to the net. Siebert cut across the ice hoping to block Richard but realized he could not get in front of the speedy Montréal forward. Arriving at Richard's side, Siebert wrapped his arms around the Rocket's shoulders to slow him down and tried to poke the puck off Richard's stick. The crowd at the Forum gasped as Siebert ended up on Richard's back. In the stunned silence of the Forum, the fans could hear the sound of the Rocket's skates rasping against the ice as he bore the extra weight on his back. Apparently, nothing was going to stop Maurice as he entered the Red Wings' defensive zone.

"I felt as if I might cave in. The goaltender moved straight out for me, and somehow I managed to jab the puck between his legs while Siebert kept riding my back!" exclaimed Richard after the game.

In the Detroit locker room, Coach Jack Adams laid into his defenceman for not stopping Richard on the play. Siebert replied, "Listen, Mr. Adams.

I weigh over 200 pounds. Any guy who can carry me on his back from the blue line to the net deserves to score a goal."

After that game, Richard was a fan favourite. If he could set a 50-goal record, he would become a legend.

By March 1945, Richard had reached 49 goals. Fans were waiting to see if he could reach 50 before the season wrapped up. The Canadiens were playing the Boston Bruins on March 18, 1945, in the final game of the season. Richard knew this was his last chance to score the goal. If he didn't, his 49 goals in the season would be only a side note in the hockey history books.

By the end of the second period, it looked as if Richard would not get his record-setting goal. With the score 3–2 in favour of the Habs near the end of the third period, the Bruins were playing a tight game. Richard's teammates knew his chances to score were dwindling. They did everything possible to help him get his 50th goal. With just over two minutes left, Richard got a chance.

Rushing across the blue line, Richard and Elmer Lach set their sights on Boston goaltender Harvey Bennett. Trying to draw Bennett and the defenceman away from Richard, Lach cut in front of the net and tried to feather a pass to the Rocket. A Bruins defenceman crashed into Lach. Their momentum carried them into the goaltender, who was pushed away from the front of the goal. Somehow the puck found its way onto Richard's stick, and he poked it into the empty net for his 50th goal. Bennett immediately ran to the referee to protest that Lach had purposely interfered with him in the crease but had no luck convincing the officials of the obstruction. The goal stood! The Canadiens players swarmed around their new star player. Québec's new hero had done it.

Author Roch Carrier described the feeling of the Québec fans well when he wrote, "When Richard scored his 50 goals, he gave us all hope. French Canadians are no longer to be condemned to be hewers of wood and drawers of water, to be servants, employees. We, too, are champions of the world."

It wasn't until the 1980–81 season that New York Islanders Mike Bossy equalled Richard's 50-in-50 achievement, and in December 1981, Wayne Gretzky smashed the record by scoring 50 goals in 39 games.

The Masked Jacques Plante

Standing in front of a frozen piece of speeding rubber with nothing to protect your face is considered crazy nowadays, but before Jacques Plante donned a mask it was all in a day's work for a goaltender to wear nothing on his face but a determined look.

The first professional hockey player to wear a mask was Clint Benedict of the Montréal Maroons. He wore a crude leather mask for a short time in 1930 after his nose was broken by one of Howie Morenz's hard shots. However, he quickly decided not to continue wearing it, because it blocked his vision. No other goaltender wore a mask regularly during games until Jacques Plante defied convention and the urging of his coach.

Goaltenders were made of tough stuff in the early days of the National Hockey League. They often played every game of the season and teams did not have a back-up goaltender to replace them if they were injured or having a bad game. They had to contend with players crashing into the net, sticks catching them in the face and speeding pucks. Not having a mask forced goaltenders to use an upright style of goaltending. Only the bravest or craziest of goaltenders crouched low and exposed their faces to speeding pucks. Terry Sawchuk, for example, was one of those low-crouching goalies. His face displayed the price he paid, with more than 400 stitches during his career.

It was considered a sign of weakness for a goaltender to wear a mask. Even though Plante often wore a mask during practice, Canadiens coach Toe Blake, who did not get along with the eccentric Plante, forbade him to wear it during regular games for fear Plante would be thought puck shy.

"If you wear it when the season starts and have a bad game, the fans will blame the mask and get on you," counselled Blake.

Plante had many reasons for insisting on wearing a mask. In 1954, his right cheekbone was fractured during practice by a shot from teammate Bert Olmstead. The injury sidelined him for five weeks. In 1955, Don Marshall sidelined him again for five weeks when he broke Plante's left cheekbone and nose on a shot during practice. After those incidents, Plante began wearing a mask during practice but never in games because it cut his vision too much.

"I kept it on religiously in practices from then on," said Plante in Andy O'Brien's book *The Jacques Plante Story*, "wondering all the while about what kind of a mask would be practical for wearing in games."

The mask he was looking for did not appear until 1958 when Bill Burchmore, a salesman from Fiberglass Canada Limited, approached him with a design for a mask that would mould to his face and allow him to see without obstruction. The finished product was thin, padded and tough as steel. In it, Plante looked rather scary. His eyes stared through two holes in the pale flesh-coloured form. Coach Blake would not budge, however, and did not allow his goaltender to wear the mask during a game. Blake said he feared that Plante would not be able to see the puck and thought wearing masks was something that just wasn't done in the NHL. He changed his mind on November 1, 1959.

That night the Canadiens were playing the New York Rangers. Just a few minutes into the first period, Rangers forward Andy Bathgate broke in from the left wing, got within five metres of the net and took a hard rising shot right into Plante's nose. The referee saw Plante go down and whistled the play dead. Plante lay on the ice, out cold from the pain, his blood slowly pooling on the ice around him. After he was taken off the ice and stitched up by the Rangers' physician, Jacques secretly smiled to himself because he now had an excuse to use his mask, and his coach would not stop him.

Taking one look at his goaltender's broken and bloody face, Blake conceded defeat, "Wear your mask if you want, Jacques." The Canadiens won that game 3–1 and won the next 11 games. Plante had won the argument with his coach.

Still some people were slow to get used to the idea of masked goaltenders. In an article published in *Modern Man Magazine* of 1960, Arturo F. Gonzales wrote of Plante's appearance, "Crouched in the cage with the sun-white glare of hockey rink floodlights carving his artificial 'face' into deeply shadowed eye sockets and a gaping hole of a 'mouth,' Plante looks like something out of a Hollywood horror film. And when he uncoils and catapults from his cage toward an opposing player…his image stirs butterflies in the stomach of his target." Although this is a tad overdramatized, his sentiment is clear.

The hard shots of players such as Bernie Geoffrion and Bobby Hull made masks necessities for modern goaltenders, but it took one person to stand up to convention and make history.

Bill Barilko's Final Goal

Hockey has had a lot of heroes, but none received hero status faster than a young Toronto Maple Leafs defenceman named Bill Barilko. After only five seasons in the NHL with the Leafs, Barilko was recognized as a solid defenceman but was known for his thundering body checks more than his scoring ability. Despite this, a goal he scored in the 1951 Stanley Cup finals earned him a place among the greatest players in National Hockey League history.

The Maple Leafs were up 3–1 on the Montréal Canadiens in the Stanley Cup finals. They wanted to wrap up the series in Toronto before Montréal had a chance to rebound on home ice. The series could have gone either way. Each game finished in overtime with the Leafs coming out on the winning side thanks to heroics from players like Sid Smith and Ted Kennedy.

Game five was no different than the previous four games. With the Canadiens leading 2–1 and the seconds ticking away, Leafs coach Joe Primeau pulled goaltender Al Rollins and prayed his team could tie the score and send the game into overtime. He got his wish when Tod Sloan fought his way to the front of the Montréal goal and picked up a rebound from Canadiens netminder Gerry McNeil. The Leafs tied the game with just 32 seconds left on the clock.

Primeau, nervous during the sudden-death overtime, wanted his team to play it safe. He instructed his defencemen to stay at the blue lines ready to fall back at the first sign of a Canadiens' attack to prevent Montréal's speedy forwards, such as Maurice Richard and Bernie Geoffrion, from rushing in on two-on-one attacks. Luckily one Leafs defenceman did not take instruction well.

Two minutes had passed when the Leafs broke into the Canadiens' zone and set up a perimeter around Montréal goaltender Gerry McNeil. When a shot bounced off McNeil, Barilko darted in from the blue line and flipped the puck over the prostrate Montréal goaltender. At just 2:53 of extra time, Bill Barilko won the Leafs the Cup. The Leafs celebrated their Stanley Cup by parading Barilko around the Maple Leaf Gardens on their shoulders.

Although he had given his team the Cup, Barilko's play was dangerous and could have backfired on the team. "For our defencemen to be as deep as he was, at that point of the game, was dangerous," said teammate Howie Meeker. "But that was Barilko."

That summer was full of celebration for Barilko. He was a hero to the people of Toronto. Unfortunately, this was his last brush with glory. To end the summer, he and his buddy Henry Hudson decided to get a little relaxation by flying up north to spend the weekend fishing. They were last seen flying near James Bay on their way south, but they never arrived at their destination.

Leafs' owner Conn Smythe offered a $10,000 reward for anyone who had information leading to the whereabouts of Barilko, but it seemed no one knew what had happened to the young defenceman. As time passed, rumours were bandied about that Barilko was teaching hockey in Russia or smuggling gold in Northern Ontario. Eventually, the search was called off.

The mystery of Barilko's disappearance was solved 11 years later, in 1962, when a provincial forestry department pilot was flying near Cochrane, Ontario, and saw sunlight reflecting off a piece of metal in the overgrown forest. When authorities travelled on foot to the area, they found Barilko's plane with two skeletons still strapped in their seats.

Was it coincidence or just plain bad luck that during the years when Barilko's fate was unknown, the Leafs did not do well and on several occasions did not even make the playoffs. It wasn't until the wreckage was found that the Leafs won the Stanley Cup again.

A picture of Barilko and his sweater (number 5) still hangs in the home of the Toronto Maple Leafs to help us remember a Stanley Cup hero and a life taken too early.

Bill Mosienko's 3-in-21

In the early 1950s, the Chicago Blackhawks were at the bottom of the league and had been struggling for several years. They suffered from a lack of public support that saw many seats empty for their home games. The team had little success until Bobby Hull captured glory for the team several years later. In 1952, Chicago fans were eager for any sort of victory, and their captain Bill Mosienko provided one of the greatest moments in goal-scoring history.

His moment of glory came on the last night of the season when in front of a small crowd of just 3000 at Madison Square Garden, the last-place Chicago Blackhawks faced off against the fifth-place New York Rangers. The game did not mean anything in the standings. Both teams had been eliminated from the playoffs and were only playing to end the season on a high note.

The quiet crowd was treated to an open-ended game with both teams getting their fair chances on net. By the end of the second period, the Rangers had come out on top with 5 goals to Chicago's 2. Chicago coach Eddie Goodfellow paced the locker room, searching his mind for some inspirational words to motivate his team.

"I know this hasn't been the greatest season, guys, but this doesn't mean we have to give up. The Rangers aren't any better than we are. They are playing the type of game that we thrive in, so why aren't we the ones with the lead?" Goodfellow argued. "All we need to do is start connecting some passes and running our system, and things will definitely turn our way. Heck! I'll even bet my job on it!"

At the six-minute mark of the third period after a further Ranger goal, things began to turn around for the Hawks. After a faceoff in their own zone, Blackhawks centre Gus Bodnar caught Mosienko with a pass up centre ice. Mosienko made his way through the neutral zone and blasted a shot from the Rangers' blue line, beating the stunned Rangers goaltender Lorne Anderson at 6:09. At the centre-ice faceoff following the goal, Mosienko got the puck. He cut across the blue line in front of the goalie and let loose a shot that found the back of the net at 6:20. The quiet crowd suddenly awoke at the two quick goals by the Blackhawks captain.

His third goal was a carbon copy of his second. Mosienko got the puck after the faceoff, made his way into the Rangers' zone and fired a shot from the top of the circle that beat the Rangers goalie at 6:30. Mosienko had scored a hat trick in 21 seconds, destroying the old record of one minute and four seconds set by Detroit Red Wings' Carl Liscombe in 1938.

The Blackhawks took advantage of their momentum and beat the Rangers with a final score of 7–6. After the game, coach Goodfellow congratulated Mosienko on his performance.

"Must have been my little speech that inspired you, eh, Mosy!" said Goodfellow jokingly.

"Yeah, must have been!" said Mosienko with a smile on his face.

(Ironically, although Chicago won the game, Eddie Goodfellow never coached again in the NHL.)

Breaking the Colour Barrier: Willie O'Ree

He had been waiting all his life for the moment he first put on the Boston Bruins jersey. Now he could call himself a professional hockey player. He had first put on a pair of skates at the age of three and had been dreaming of this moment ever since. But the road to the NHL was not an easy one for a black hockey player during the 1950s and 1960s.

It seems ridiculous today that a player would be excluded on the sole condition of the colour of his skin, but that was the attitude in the days before Willie O'Ree broke into the NHL. There were plenty of black players in the minor hockey leagues around North America, but none had broken into the NHL.

Young Toronto-born Herb Carnegie, who in the 1940s played in the Québec Senior Hockey League for the Québec Aces, was recognized as one of the best players on his team but was denied the chance of trying out for an NHL club only because of his skin colour. Toronto Maple Leafs' owner Conn Smythe even told the young player, "Herb, I'd sign you in a minute if I could turn you white." The talent was there; however, management lacked the will to break the colour barrier.

O'Ree finally got a chance when the Boston Bruins called him up from the minors for two games played against the Montréal Canadiens starting on January 18, 1958. He did not score during this brief stay with the Bruins, but he changed the game forever. Like Jackie Robinson had done 10 years earlier in major-league baseball, O'Ree broke the NHL's colour barrier. However, it still wasn't easy to be black in the National Hockey League.

"I know Robinson had it much tougher," said O'Ree

O'Ree was called up to the Bruins again three years later for the last half of the 1960–61 season. This time O'Ree moved with the team as it travelled to other cities and found himself accepted into the team. However, during these "away" games, racial slurs were thrown at him almost every night.

"They were mean to me in places like Detroit and New York, too. But never in Boston," said O'Ree in Brian McFarlane's book *Best of the Original Six*. "I'll never forget how my teammates there—men like Johnny Bucyk, Doug Mohns, Charlie Burns and Don McKenney—took care of me. They accepted me totally. All of them had class."

When asked about the new addition to the team, Bruins coach Milt Schmidt said, "He isn't black. He's a Bruin."

Players on other teams were not welcoming to the black player. They taunted O'Ree about his colour. Fans cursed at him every time he touched the puck. One night in Chicago the taunting got out of hand after an incident involving O'Ree and Blackhawks forward Eric Nesterenko.

Trouble started when Nesterenko went into the corner to check O'Ree off the puck. The butt-end of his stick went right into O'Ree's mouth and knocked out two of his teeth. After O'Ree retaliated by banging Nesterenko on the head with his stick, the crowd hurled racial slurs at the bleeding Boston defenceman. The referee threw both players out of the game. O'Ree had trouble getting off the ice, because fans were throwing anything they could get their hands on at him. O'Ree needed a police escort to usher him off the ice and out of the arena. The game was stopped to prevent any further violence.

"Those Chicago fans were livid. They were ready to murder me," said O'Ree.

O'Ree played only 45 games with the Boston Bruins before being traded to the Montréal Canadiens, where he did not get any ice time. He spent the rest of his career in the minor leagues where he twice won the Western Hockey League scoring title.

By crossing the colour line, O'Ree paved the way for kids who might never have got the chance to play in the NHL.

Bob Baun: With One Leg to Stand on

People in hockey, especially Don Cherry, love to talk about how hockey players are the toughest athletes in professional sports. No one fits the description better than Saskatchewan-born Toronto Maple Leafs defenceman Bob Baun.

A solid defenceman but not an offensive threat, a highlight of Baun's career came in 1964 when the Leafs faced off against the Detroit Red Wings in the Stanley Cup finals. After game five, the Red Wings led the series three games to two. The Leafs needed to win both of the remaining games to take the Cup back to Toronto for a third straight year. About halfway through the third period of game six with the score tied at 3, Gordie Howe crossed the red line and blasted a shot that found its way onto the small unpadded area between the skate boot and the shin guard of Leafs defenceman Bob Baun.

"I heard a boom like an cannon. It was the bone cracking," said Baun

Trying to stay in position as the Red Wings pressed into the zone, Baun stumbled and fell to the ice in extreme pain. Carried off the ice on a stretcher, Baun's injured leg was taped and frozen by the club doctor. With the score tied at the end of the third period, the game went into overtime. Baun returned to the Leafs' bench ready to assume his duties on the blue line. It proved to be a great decision for the team.

It wasn't the prettiest of goals, but Baun didn't complain. After intercepting a Red Wings' pass, Baun fired the puck into the Wings' zone. It hit a defenceman's stick and bounced past the goaltender, winning the game for the Leafs and sending the series to Toronto for game seven.

After the game Baun was noticeably wincing in pain but refused to admit that he should not play in game seven. He avoided team physicians so that he would not have to undergo an x-ray on his leg. Teammates knew something was wrong as Baun limped around the locker room before the start of game seven. They said nothing for fear that drawing attention to his injury might force Baun to miss out on the final game in the Stanley Cup series.

Despite his injury, Baun suited up for game seven and played his regular shifts. The Leafs won the game 4–0, and the Stanley Cup for the third year in a row. After the celebrations died down, Baun finally agreed to an x-ray. The film confirmed what he already knew—he had played two games with a broken shinbone.

Explaining his ability to play despite the pain of a broken leg, Baun said, "I guess it was my pain tolerance and the mental ability to block things out."

After the story got out, coaches around the league were heard to say to their injured players, "If Baun can play on a broken leg, what's your excuse?"

Bobby Orr Takes Flight

Defencemen have a specific job to do. They rarely take up offensive positions and usually hold the back line to prevent rushes up their end of the ice. Top defencemen, such as Doug Harvey and Pierre Pilote, play their positions perfectly. Their offensive abilities were only displayed during power plays or odd-man rushes. With Bobby Orr, defencemen and coaches around the league began to rethink the traditional role of defencemen.

In his first season with the Bruins, Orr won rookie-of-the-year honours and sent coaches and managers around the league scrambling to find defensive talent as imaginative as Orr. In the 1969–70 season, both Orr and the Bruins went straight to the top of the League.

While Orr was not the first defenceman to rush into the offensive zone with the puck, he was the first to use his offensive skills on a regular basis and with such outstanding success. Most teams had never seen a defenceman with an offensive side. They had a hard time containing Orr in one corner of the rink. Boston fans held their breath in anticipation as Orr wound up in his zone, gaining speed with his long strides, then rushed to the other end of the rink untouched to score a goal or make a beautiful pass.

As memorable as his offensive skills were, Orr was also no defensive slouch. As quickly as he skated into the offensive zone, he skated back to cover his position and stop the other team from getting a shot off on his goaltender.

"I played a style that players and coaches were not accustomed to seeing," said Orr. "I was not meant to sit on the blue line and would have suffered if the Bruins had ordered me to sit back."

By combining the rushing defensive talents of Orr and the goal-scoring talents of Phil Esposito, Boston head coach Harry Sinden created one of the most effective teams in the NHL at the time, strong and powerful both on defence and offence. Orr finished the regular season with a record-breaking 120 points and the distinction of being the first-ever defenceman to win the scoring title. All the Bruins had to do was prove themselves in the playoffs.

The Bruins had built a solid team around their young defenceman and looked promising going into the playoffs. They had a little difficulty knocking off the New York Rangers but easily handled the Chicago Blackhawks in the semi-finals. Moving on to the finals, they faced the St. Louis Blues for the Cup.

In the finals against the Blues, the Bruins won the first three games. If the Bruins could win the fourth game, they would win the Cup. In game four, at the end of the third period, the score was tied. The game went into overtime.

It is one of the most famous pictures in hockey history. It captures what every young player dreams of doing if he can make it to the NHL: scoring a goal in overtime to win the Stanley Cup.

"Seeing the famous photograph of me flying through the air after scoring the overtime goal to give the Boston Bruins the 1970 Stanley Cup brings back a flood of memories," said Bobby Orr in the book *For the Love of Hockey*. "I remember the thrill of getting that goal and the good fortune of being part of that special team. When I was a boy, I watched in awe as the Stanley Cup was carried high over the shoulders of the winning team, and today, that photograph represents the excitement of realizing that dream."

Many have seen the photo of Orr flying through the air, arms high above his head in celebration after scoring the overtime goal to win the Stanley Cup. To those who watched the goal live, it felt like time stood still.

The winning play began with a brilliant pass from Bruins' tough guy Derek Sanderson who spotted Orr making his way in front of St. Louis Blues goaltender Glenn Hall. Orr skated across the front of the net, forcing Hall to commit to a shot prematurely, and put the puck underneath the sprawled-out goaltender. Blues defenceman Noel Picard, tried to stop Orr but was just a fraction of a second too late. As Orr's shot went home, Picard upended Orr and sent him flying through the air. Overcome with emotion at having scored the winning goal in the Stanley Cup finals, Bobby Orr raised his arms in triumph as he flew through the air, seemingly unaware that the ice was quickly rushing up at him.

"I always tell Bobby he was up in the air for so long that I had time to shower and change before he hit the ice," said Glenn Hall, recalling the famous goal.

Next season Orr improved his scoring totals and finished the season with 139 points, the most ever by a defenceman. The only other defenceman to come close was Edmonton's Paul Coffee who ended the 1985–86 season with 138 points.

Orr won the Stanley Cup with the Bruins again in 1972 and was handed the Hart Trophy as the league's most valuable player and the Norris Trophy as the league's top defenceman.

Orr's time at the top though was shortened by a recurring knee injury. With each passing year, Orr's knees deteriorated to the point where he could no longer effectively play his position. The famous end-to-end rushes were not happening as frequently as they once did. He had one last moment in the spotlight when he represented Canada at the 1976 Canada Cup. It was the last time Bobby Orr skated with the grace and skill that he had when he had led his team to two Stanley Cup victories.

"Following the Canada Cup, I played a few games for the Chicago Blackhawks, took a year off to recuperate and played a few more games before it was readily apparent that my leg bothered me too much. My game was skating, and my knee would no longer hold up," said Orr, looking back at the end of his career.

After only nine full seasons in the NHL, Orr was forced to retire from the game he loved at the young age of 31. One can only guess what his career would have been like if he had not been plagued by injuries.

Sittler Scores a Perfect 10

February 7, 1976. The Toronto Maple Leafs played the Boston Bruins in a game that would establish their position in the playoffs. No one expected the game to be a high-scoring affair, but Leafs captain Darryl Sittler didn't get the memo. Sittler's scoring run started off slowly in the first period with two assists and then continued with a hat trick in the second. Boston coach Don Cherry decided to leave his rookie goaltender Dave Reece in the net to face the music. By the end of the third period, Sittler had added another hat trick and an assist on a fluke goal when the puck bounced off Brad Park's skate and went into the net. By the end of the night Sittler had a record 10-point game, and the Leafs naturally won the game 11–4. The Boston goaltender was dubbed "In-the-wrong-place-at-the-wrong-time" Reece.

"As much as the fans fault Reece for what happened, it was simply a night where every shot and pass I made seemed to pay off in a goal," said Sittler. "I hit the corners a couple of times, banking shots in off the post. The kid was screened on a couple of goals and had no chance. He didn't really flub one goal."

Wayne Gretzky Breaks Them All

With 61 National Hockey League records held or shared and a career filled with amazing plays, it's difficult to single out one moment that can be defined as Wayne Gretzky's greatest.

Wayne Gretzky had been breaking records since he started playing hockey. While he was not yet a teenager, he scored 378 goals in 82 games. Everyone watching the skinny kid from Brantford, Ontario, knew that he was destined for hockey greatness. The time he spent on the backyard rink practicing his shooting and skating and visualizing how the game is played was paying off for the young phenom. Some nights his father strapped on his skates and braved the cold to teach his son the few things he knew about hockey.

"Parents come up to me now saying, 'We'd like you to tell our son that he has to practice hockey the way you did, for six, seven or eight hours a day.' I tell them that's not my philosophy," said Gretzky. "It really wasn't practice—it was fun. I enjoyed myself. If I had considered it practice, I would not have done it."

When Gretzky outgrew the backyard rink, he made his way to the professional ranks at 17 years of age. The sports world was waiting to see what the young prodigy could do. Gretzky knew he had the talent to play in the NHL, and that his small size wouldn't matter. However, Gretzky took the criticism of his detractors to heart, and like a true champion, he used the doubts to motivate himself. In his first season with the new franchise Edmonton Oilers, Gretzky scored 51 goals and 86 assists for a total of 137 points.

He wasn't a power forward like Gordie Howe or a sniper like Bobby Hull. Gretzky brought a different approach to the game that made him just as effective, or even more so, than previous NHL scoring stars. On teams with players like Howe or Hull, players desperate for a goal would try to get the puck to the big scorers. Other teams, of course, knew this, so they designated two players to shadow the stars to prevent breakaway goals or open shots on net. Realizing that Gretzky was a scoring threat, coaches tried to contain him using the old system of having one or two players shadow Gretzky during offensive rushes. Gretzky's small size meant he wasn't able to muscle his way past two defencemen while shaking another player off his back.

Instead, Gretzky was able to take advantage of the situation. Having the attention focused on him, the ice was open for other players on his line. With trademark passes, Gretzky was often able to feed these open players. Not only did Gretzky score a prodigious amount of points, but the other players on the ice with him also benefited from his style of play.

The 1981–82 season was Gretzky's breakout year, the one when he established his name. At the tender age of 20, Gretzky was on track not only to break but to shatter Maurice Richard's 50-goals-in-50-games record set in 1944–45, which had been equalled for the first time only the year before by Mike Bossy. Although averaging even 1 goal per game was hard, Gretzky destroyed the record.

When Gretzky reached 45 goals in 38 games, everybody knew he would break Richard's record, but expected it might take him 45 or 48 games to do it. No one watching the game between the Oilers and the Philadelphia Flyers on the night of December 30, 1981 expected Gretzky to score five goals and beat the record in a mere 39 games. But the Flyers were a team of large relatively slow players who had difficulty containing the speedy Oilers. Gretzky ran away with the game, scoring the five goals he needed for the record.

After the history-making goal near the end of the game, the media swarmed Gretzky, shooting questions at him.

"Gretzky! Wayne!" yelled one reporter to get Gretzky's attention. "What does it feel like to break such a coveted record?"

"Now that you have 50 goals in 39 games do you think you'll break Esposito's 76 regular season goals?" asked another reporter.

Gretzky responded calmly, "To hit 76, I'd have to get 26 goals in 40 games. Never mind what's happened up 'til now; that's a lot of goals. I still have a long way to go, and I will not make any predictions. Now, if you guys will excuse me I have to call my dad."

Despite his expectations, Gretzky finished the season with 92 goals and 120 assists for another record-breaking total of 212 points. The records continued to fall over the years, as Gretzky moved closer to Gordie Howe's career-goal total, which many people thought impossible to break.

Playing for the Los Angeles Kings after the infamous trade in 1988, Gretzky broke the record for all-time points in regular season play in 1989. His sights then were set on the career-goal record.

Gretzky broke that record on March 23, 1994, when the Kings played the Vancouver Canucks before a crowd of 16,000 plus fans packed into Los Angeles' Great Western Forum. Fans showed up in droves wanting to see their hockey hero break Howe's career-goal mark of 801. The moment came in the second period on a rush started by Luc Robitaille with Marty McSorley and Gretzky following close behind. Robitaille carried the puck into the Vancouver zone and passed it to Gretzky who had McSorley with him for a two-on-one. Gretzky hit McSorley with a pass. McSorley could have shot on net but instead passed it back to Gretzky who had the open net and shovelled it in for his 802nd goal.

"When I got the puck back, I saw the whole net," said Gretzky after the game. "I couldn't believe I saw it."

The game was stopped for 10 minutes to honour the momentous occasion with a brief ceremony. Despite all the records and Stanley Cup wins, the goal was one of the most memorable moments in Gretzky's career.

NHL Commissioner Gary Bettman put it well when he said, "You have always been the 'Great One' but tonight you are the greatest."

Mario the Magnificent
Scores for the Cycle

On December 30, 1988, Mario Lemieux scored five goals against the New Jersey Devils. As amazing as a five-goal game is, scoring each goal in a different way is incredible. Lemieux scored a power play goal, scored when his team was short-handed and even-strength, scored on an empty net and scored with a penalty shot. No one has equalled or come close to scoring for the cycle. That's why he was named "The Magnificent."

Honourable Mention: Bourque Wins Cup, Finally!

To hold the Stanley Cup above your head is the dream of every hockey player. However, the Cup can be elusive. For many NHL players the dream never comes true. Imagine years of physical and mental training; imagine spending your whole life with one goal in mind—and then never achieving that goal.

Ray Bourque's career was marked with achievement, awards and records, but the big prize eluded him during his 20 years as a Boston Bruin defenceman. Bourque didn't have many seasons left in him and predicted that the Bruins were not going to win the Stanley Cup any time soon. To hold the Stanley Cup above his head, he had to join a new team that had a chance at making it into the playoffs. Transferring to another team wasn't an easy decision for the long-time Bruins defenceman. The city of Boston and the team had been good to him over the years, and it was hard to imagine Bourque in any other sweater other than a Bruins jersey.

Looking around the NHL for a possible team, Bourque quickly set his sights on the Colorado Avalanche. His first season with the team, 1999–2000, ended when Dallas eliminated Colorado in the playoffs. The next season Colorado finished the season at the top of the league with 118 points. Bourque felt confident about his team's chances when the team went into the playoffs to face the Vancouver Canucks in the first-round conference quarterfinals.

"I feel really good about how I fit in, and I've been hoping and thinking that things might work out this way," said Bourque in an interview with Nancy Marrapese-Burrell of ESPN.com.

All he needed was 16 wins, and the Cup would be his, but of course the Cup does not come easily. Although Colorado beat the Canucks in a four-game sweep, they had a difficult time disposing of the Los Angeles Kings and only prevailed against the St. Louis Blues after another hard-fought series. The Avalanche ended up in the Stanley Cup final against the defending champions, the New Jersey Devils.

The series looked to be a hard-fought affair. The Devils had finished just a few points behind the Avalanche during the regular season. The teams had the all-star goaltending talents of the Devils' Martin Brodeur and the Avalanche's Patrick Roy.

After five games, the Devils had the lead in the series, up 3–2. Bourque was worried he would not get to hold the Stanley Cup. Game six was a turnaround for the Avalanche. They shut out the Devils 4–0. Bourque and the Avalanche went into game seven confident they could steal the Cup away from New Jersey.

On June 9, 2001, Bourque finally got what he had been chasing for 22 long years. At the end of the game, the score was 3–1 in favour of the Avalanche.

Bourque's moment had finally arrived. In a show of class, after being presented the Cup, captain Joe Sakic immediately handed it to Bourque. Bourque kissed it and lifted it up above his head with a tear in his eye and the biggest smile in the arena. Even as he celebrated winning the Cup with the Avalanche, his mind was on his former team.

"I can't say enough about Boston. I had two cracks at the Cup there. Everyone I played with there has a little piece of this," he added after the game.

"What a way to end a career," Colorado defenceman Rob Blake said after game seven.

"It would have been a shame if Ray had left the game without a Stanley Cup," said Colorado forward Peter Forsberg.

A few weeks later, having accomplished what he had set out to do, Bourque, finally a Stanley Cup champion, announced his retirement from the NHL.

Chapter Three

Greatest Moments in International Hockey

Summit Series: Paul Henderson's Moment of Glory

Canadians have always thought of themselves as having the best hockey players in the world. It was on the frozen ponds of eastern Canada that the game of hockey was first played, so one must assume that Canadians are the best, right? Canada had dominated the first 30 years of Winter Olympic competition, but when they went into the 1972 Summit Series they had not won a gold medal since the 1952 Olympic Games.

By 1972, the USSR was becoming recognized as a hockey powerhouse. Soviet hockey players had won several world championships as well as gold medals at the Winter Olympics on several occasions. When the opportunity came to have the National Hockey League's best players take on the talent of the Soviet Union, the media predicted the eight-game series would end in a sweep in favour of the talent-filled Canadian roster. Across Canada, hockey fans placed a lot of pride in the Canadian team that would face off against the Russians in the 1972 Summit Series. The pride of two hockey nations were on the line, and each player knew the significance of the series and the political subtext attached to the games.

"The country's at stake here," said Phil Esposito, never one at loss for the dramatic. "I mean, that's my thought. It's our society at stake against theirs."

The Montréal Forum played host to the first game in the much-anticipated series. Politicians from both countries, including the Soviet ambassador to Canada and Prime Minister Pierre Elliot Trudeau, were on hand to watch the teams do battle. Team Canada came onto the ice to thunderous applause from the Forum crowd. With players like Phil Esposito, Yvan Cournoyer, Frank and Peter Mahovlich, Serge Savard and, in goal, Ken Dryden and Tony Esposito, the crowd expected an outstanding performance against the Russian team.

The reception for the Russians was less warm when they hit the ice. They wore red CCCP jerseys and overwhelmed expressions on their faces.

"Before that first game we had a very nervous feeling," recalled Soviet player Boris Mikhailov. "It was scary. We just wanted to begin playing."

The Soviets' nervousness allowed Canada to score 2 goals in the first few minutes of the opening period. The Forum went wild after the second goal. The Canadian crowd relaxed in their seats, believing their team could easily handle the obviously unprepared Russian squad.

The second goal by the Canadians seemed to wake the Russians from their daze. They took control of the pace of the game. At just over the halfway point in the first period, they got their first goal. The mood in the Forum quickly changed from confidence to worry.

Canada seemed to be scrambling to keep up with the speedy Soviet forwards. When a Russian scored a short-handed goal in the closing minutes of the first period, Team Canada lost the confidence it had during the opening minutes. The second and third periods brought no luck to the Canadians. The Russian added to their lead and finished the game with a shocking 7–3 victory. In the dressing room after the game, the Canadians had time to brood about how seriously they had misjudged the Soviets' talent.

"At that point, there was an absolutely sickening feeling," recalled Henderson, speaking of the second-period Russian goals. "We all knew that the sleeping giant had been awoken, and we were going to have a fight on our hands."

Team Canada was out-skated, out-hustled and repeatedly frustrated by the Soviet team and the daring acrobatic talents of its young Russian goaltender, Vladislav Tretiak. Despite the excuses the Canadian team used to explain away their embarrassing first-game loss to the Soviets, in game two, they needed to prove to themselves and the world that they would not be beaten easily.

Before game two at Maple Leaf Gardens, Canadian coach Harry Sinden gathered his team in the dressing room. He scanned the downhearted group of men that now wore nervous looks on their faces similar to those worn by the Russians at the beginning of game one. With the passion of a preacher, Sinden tried to restore his team's faith and conviction that was so abundant before the start of the series. It seemed to work.

Canada came out at the start of the game with a strategy of aggressively forechecking the speedy Russian forwards and preventing them from grouping for attacks into the Canadian zone. The plan seemed to work, and the Canadians took control of the game. With some solid goaltending from Tony Esposito, Canada came away from game two with a victory. They had tied the series up at a game apiece. Canada had regained its confidence. This time they were not going to let overconfidence get the best of them.

The Canadians played the third game with the same strategy they had used in game two: stay close to the guy with the puck; forecheck aggressively;

stay alert on the man-to-man coverage thereby cancelling the Soviets' speed and their ability to adapt, the skills that allowed them to initiate odd-man rushes. In this game, Team Canada played better than before, but the Soviets matched everything the Canadians threw at them. The game ended in a tie.

Although it was a tie, it felt like a loss to the Canadians. Dissension tore away at the team.

"We were having problems on the ice; some guys were complaining about not playing; and we always seemed to have a different lineup each game," said Yvan Cournoyer. "It just never seemed to work as well as it could."

Emotions reached a fever pitch before the start of game four in Vancouver. The media questioned the abilities of the Canadian team, and the public's confidence in their hockey heroes began to wane. Since Canada was not accustomed to playing against the Soviet system of hockey, they were slow to figure out how to overcome it. The media had aroused the public, who were starting to complain about the embarrassing way the Soviets were beating the Canadians at their own game. The media second-guessed the coach and players on every decision. Some media were already sounding the death knell of the Canadian hockey team.

As the teams took to the ice for game four, discontent was palpable among the 15,000 fans that packed the Pacific Coliseum. It didn't take long for the crowd to turn against the first Canadian player to show weakness on the ice. This chilly reception caught Team Canada off guard. The Soviets quickly took advantage of the Canadians' skittish play and ended the first period up 2–0. The game did not improve for the Canadians in the second and third periods. The Russians dominated and, with a solid performance from Tretiak, ended game four with a 5–3 victory. Upset at the loss, the crowd at the Pacific Coliseum booed their team for its poor performance. They were let down by their country's best—they felt they had a right to vent their anger.

Paul Henderson remembered turning to Phil Esposito during the second intermission. Henderson was upset at his own performance and distraught by the chilly reception from the fans. He said to Esposito, "Our own people are turning on us." To which Esposito replied, "I hope that I'm picked the star of the game because I'm really going to give them a piece of my mind tonight. I've had enough of this."

As the Canadian players slowly skated off the ice with their heads hung low in disappointment, Esposito walked to the nearest camera and vented his anger in what turned out to be a memorable moment in Canadian hockey.

Upset and emotionally overcome, Esposito stared into the camera and delivered an honest response to the harsh criticism levelled against his team.

"To the people across Canada, we're trying our best. For the people who booed us, geez, I'm really...all of the guys are really disheartened and we're disillusioned and disappointed in some of the people. We cannot believe the bad press we've got...the booing in our own buildings. Every one of us guys, 35 guys who came out to play for Team Canada, we did it because we love our country and not for any other reason....And even though we play in the United States and we earn money in the United States, Canada is still our home, and that's the only reason we come. And I don't think it's fair that we should be booed." With those final words to the country, Team Canada left for the Soviet Union to play the remaining four games.

Although they lost game five, Team Canada found the confidence it needed in the ·Soviet Union, where it was isolated from the scrutiny of the Canadian sports media. They won the next two games and tied the series. The team that won the last game of the series would be able to claim they were the best in the world.

September 28, 1972. The final game. Everything that had happened in the series so far didn't matter—it all came down to this one game. The Canadian players knew this would be one of the most important games of their lives. So did the Russians. Judging by what the teams had been through, this series seemed to be more about winning a war than a simple game. Two ways of life; two ways of playing the game—only one team would come out of the series as the champions of hockey world. These were the best players from both countries, and they were playing for keeps. Citizens of both countries crowded around their television sets and radios, waiting impatiently for the first goal of the game.

Both teams came out hard at the start of the first period. Canada found itself in penalty trouble, and the Russians capitalized with a power play goal at 3:34. The penalty box on both teams stayed warm throughout the first period as the teams traded goals, ending the period tied at two.

Canada was playing the type of game they liked. Despite bad calls by the referee that kept Canadian players in the penalty box, Team Canada kept the Russians in check and got the performance they needed from goaltender Ken Dryden.

Things went bad for the Canadians in the second period. Russians put constant pressure on the Canadian defence and managed to overcome Dryden for three more goals. Canada tried everything they could to get the puck past Soviet goalie Tretiak, but the young Russian was having a typically spectacular game, letting in only one goal. The second period ended with the Soviets leading 5–3.

Something changed between the second and third periods. The Canadians came out energized after the intermission and pressed the Russian defensive zone aggressively. Canada came within one goal of the lead at 2:27 on a goal by Phil Esposito, who knocked a pass from Peter Mahovlich out of the air and into the net behind a surprised Tretiak. The Canadian fans in attendance sensed the renewed Canadian offence and started chanting the somewhat acerbic refrain "Da, Da, Canada! Nyet, Nyet, Soviet!"

Cournoyer tied the game near the halfway mark of the third and renewed Canada's hope that they would win the series. Too quickly, only six minutes remained in the game. Canada could not afford another tie. If that happened, the Soviets would win the series on the basis of a higher goal differential. It was now or never for the Canadian players.

"I was sitting on the bench at the end of the final game, and I had a sense that I could get a goal," said Henderson. "I needed to get out there to score a goal."

Henderson got his wish. He switched places with Peter Mahovlich and was on the ice for the final shift of the game. "Destiny is a word people often use," said Henderson, looking back on the moment he made hockey history.

Hockey commentator Foster Hewitt described the action of the final minute of the game:

The Canadian Team went into a huddle there, which seems to be a little unusual. [Word Lost]…they're really fighting. The puck comes up at centre ice. Vasiliev carries it back into his zone, to Shadrin who missed it. Peter Mahovlich is at centre, driving it into the Soviet zone. Liapkin gets there first. Cournoyer just touched it. Savard, getting it at centre ice, clearing it off a skate. It goes into the Canadian zone. Yakushev, a dangerous player, is belted on that play. Cournoyer rolled it out, Vasiliev going back to get it. There's 1:02 left in the game.

A cleared pass on the far side. Liapkin rolled one to Savard. Savard clears a pass to Stapleton. He cleared the open wings to Cournoyer. Here's a shot! Henderson made a wild stab for it and fell. Here's another shot, right in front…They score! Henderson scores for Canada! And the fans and the team are going wild! Henderson, right in front of the Soviet goal with 34 seconds left in the game!

The 1980 Olympic Miracle on Ice: The United States Wins Gold

Nothing makes a better story in the sporting world than the phenomenon of the underdog winning against all odds. There is something on a primal level within us that relates to underdogs. We like to think that we can overcome the impossible, too. So it wasn't only U.S. fans, but anyone who recognizes the underdog in themselves cheering the 1980 U.S. Olympic hockey team while they worked their way toward the gold medal.

The climate around the 1980 Olympics provided the perfect backdrop to the U.S. team's run for gold. The United States was in the middle of the Iran hostage crisis; the arms race between the Soviets and the Americans was continuing at an alarming rate; and the Cold War between the two superpowers was growing colder—all this at a time when the world was supposed to come together in the spirit of cooperation and friendly competition under the banner of the Olympics. It is thus no surprise that Americans from coast to coast held their breath as the U.S. team, a bunch of college-hockey kids, took on some of the greatest hockey players in their run for the gold.

At the start of the Olympics in Lake Placid, nobody gave the young team from the United States any hope of beating powerful teams from countries like Sweden, Finland, Czechoslovakia and especially the Soviet Union. But when the upstart team from the U.S. led by university coach Herb Brooks beat the Czechs, Norwegians, Romanians and West Germans, people began to take a second look at the young upstarts. When it was announced that the U.S. would play the Soviet Union for a place in the gold-medal game, many people thought it a death knell for the U.S. team.

The Soviets had destroyed the Americans in an exhibition game 11–3 just a few days earlier. The Soviets were the picture of robotic discipline, playing an emotionless yet highly effective style of hockey that had made them international hockey champions for the past decade.

The Americans were the exact opposite of the Soviets. They were young, over-emotional and had not played together until a few weeks before the start of the Olympics. Few people gave the U.S. much hope of winning against the Soviets.

The atmosphere at the Lake Placid arena was decidedly one-sided, as the teams took to the ice with the Americans in their red, white and blue uniforms and the Soviets in red communist colours. Taunts of "Commie!" and "Robots!" began to rain down on the Soviet players whose expressionless faces did not flinch at the harsh words flung their way.

Before the start of the game, coach Brooks had a few inspiring words to motivate his team, "You were born to be hockey players. You were meant to be here. This is your moment."

The Americans surprised the Soviets, playing a physical game and not letting up on their forechecking. The Americans also needed a stellar performance from their goaltender, and Jim Craig was having the best game of his life. Soviet goaltender Vladislav Tretiak was not having the greatest game and let in 2 goals before being replaced by backup goalie Vladimir Myshkin. This seemed to spark the Soviets who pulled ahead 3–2 by the end of the second period.

In the third, the U.S. tied the game on a goal by Mark Johnston, sending the American fans wild, as they felt the game slipping from the Soviets' grasp. The winning goal came off the stick of U.S. team captain Mike Eruzione who blasted a shot from 10 metres away. It went through the pads of the surprised Soviet goaltender. To this day Tretiak says he feels that if he had not been pulled the Americans would not have won. The world was in shock that the mighty Soviets had lost to the young American amateurs, and these amateurs were as shocked as the rest of the world.

"I can't believe we beat them. I can't believe we beat them," repeated Mark Johnston. "Now we're just 60 minutes away from the gold medal. I simply can't believe it."

Just a few days later, they did it again with a three-goal third-period comeback against Finland to win the gold medal.

Broadcaster Al Michaels famously cried, "Do you believe in miracles?" after the win over the Soviets. After seeing the U.S. team beat Finland and win the first Olympic gold medal for hockey in 40 years, many did believe in miracles.

The 1987 Canada Cup

The 1987 fight for the Canada Cup was a replay of the series that had defined a nation 15 years earlier. Once again Canada found itself playing for hockey supremacy against the mighty Soviet Union. The three-game series started with the Soviets winning at the Montréal Forum in overtime on a wrist shot from Alexander Semak. Canada then won the second game in overtime on a goal from Mario Lemieux.

In the final game, the Soviets pulled ahead 3–0 in the first period, but the Canadians roared back to tie the game. The game stayed close, with the score tied at 5 going into the game's final minutes. The winning goal came with just 1:26 left to play. Dale Hawerchuk got the puck to Gretzky who, with Larry Murphy and Mario Lemieux, streaked in on an odd-man rush. Gretzky fed Lemieux a perfect pass. Lemieux slapped the puck into the top corner for the winning goal. Canada was at the top of the hockey world once again.

"I was going to [pass to] No. 66 whether he wanted it or not," said Gretzky after the game.

2002 Olympic Glory: Canada Ends 50-Year Gold Drought

When hockey was still in its infancy, Canada ruled the world's rinks. Canada won the gold medal at the 1920 Olympic games, setting the pattern for the next several decades. However, after 1952, Canadian teams did not fare well until their triumphant victory in 2002.

Nothing better illustrates Canada's global dominance of the game at the time than the Canadian team's success in the first Olympic Winter Games in 1924 at Chamonix, France. The Toronto Granites were selected to represent Canada, having won back-to-back Allan Cups and three Ontario Hockey Association championships in the early 1920s. The Granites were a tough team that had plenty of confidence going into the first Olympic Winter Games against Czechoslovakia, a squad with little experience in regular competition.

Led by Reginald "Hooley" Smith and Harry "Moose" Watson, the Canadians faced an unprepared Czechoslovakian team. The Czechs could barely control the puck for more than a few seconds, and the Canadians peppered the Czech goaltender with shot after shot. When the smoke cleared, the Canadians had potted 30 goals, and the Czechs had not managed even one. The Canadians continued their domination when they faced the Swedes and summarily beat them 20–0. The Swiss were the next to feel the Canadians' wrath, handing them a 33–0 loss in which one player, Harry Watson, scored 14 goals.

In the gold-medal game, Canada faced off against Canada's favourite international rival, the United States. Yet again, the Canadians dominated the game, putting away 6 goals against a tight U.S. defence. Canada won the first Winter Olympic gold medal and won the hearts of their European hosts who feted the champions wherever they went.

Canada's international glory continued until it was interrupted in 1936 by a British hockey team composed mostly of Canadian players. After the lull in the Olympic Games caused by World War II, Canada won the gold again in 1948.

The 1952 Games in Oslo, Norway was the next opportunity for gold. The only country to provide a challenge to the Canadian hockey team was the American team. The two teams stayed neck and neck in the standings until they played each other in the gold-medal game on February 24.

The game was a hard-fought affair. The Canadian and U.S. players bashed each other up and down the ice much to the delight of the 10,000 Norwegian fans that came out to see the game. The game ended in a 3–3 draw, giving the Canadians the gold medal on total points.

As they celebrated their hard-earned victory, little did they know that it would be 50 years before Canada would again win gold. At some

Olympics in the late 20th century, the Canadian team came as close as silver, but at others, including the 1998 Games, were not even rewarded a bronze.

After a heart-breaking loss to the Czech Republic in the 1998 Nagano Olympics, Canadian hockey fans looked to the 2002 Salt Lake City Olympics as the place for Canada to take gold. As in the 1998 Olympics, the pressure for national glory once again fell on Canada's superstar ambassador of hockey Wayne Gretzky who this time led the team not as a player but as team general manager.

Doubters, deniers and unbelievers were ready to watch the Canadians again miss Olympic gold. None felt the pressure more than the players selected to bring the title back to Canada. Led by team captain Mario Lemieux, the Canadian squad included Joe Sakic, Jerome Iginla, Paul Kariya, Steve Yzerman, Chris Pronger, Theoren Fleury, Al Macinnis and stellar goaltender Martin Brodeur. The Canadian squad was recognized as one of the top teams, though it was the Czechs and the Russians who were pre-tournament favourites.

"We all know the pressure we have here in the next 10 days," said Mario Lemieux in a Canadian Press interview, "We're all professionals here. We all know what's at stake. We have a lot of confidence in each other, and I think it's going to show over the next 10 days."

However, the tournament did not start out that way. The Canadians looked shaky in their first few games. They were beaten by the better-prepared Swedes 5–2 in the first game and seemed shaky in their 3–2 victory over perennial losers Germany. Coach Pat Quinn seemed unsure of his lineups. The players worked together poorly, as if they had not been given enough time to practice together and did not yet have a feel for the others' styles. Critics quickly lambasted the shaky Canadian start. They said the team wasn't good enough, and that the rookie talent Gretzky had gathered together could not stand the pressure of an international event such as the Olympics.

The pressure came to a head when Canada played to a 3–3 tie with the Czech Republic. The international media blasted the team for not playing up to the capabilities that its roster showed and for once again proving that Canada did not have what it takes to win on the international stage.

Players from other teams chimed in, trying to knock the team off their game. Czech winger Martin Rucinsky criticized the Canadian team after the game, "We don't care about Canada. We don't take them as the team to beat. I don't think they're even close to being the best team in the tournament. You've seen that by the scores."

Gretzky had seen and heard enough. Not one known for losing his temper, the Great One lashed out at the media and those who said his team would not make it far in the tournament.

"No one wants us to win except the guys on this team and our fans, but we're a proud team and we're still standing," said Gretzky after the game with the Czechs. "It turns my stomach to hear some of the things being said about us. To a man, every one of our guys will say how great (Dominik) Hasek or (Mats) Sundin is. I don't think we dislike the other countries nearly as much as they hate us."

Gretzky took a lot of flack for his comments, but it seemed to light a fire under the Canadian players who easily beat Belarus 7–1 in their next game before moving on to the gold-medal game versus the Olympic host United States.

Fifty years to the day, Canada was set to play the same country they played when they had last won Olympic gold. To Canadians across the country, the game meant more than a gold in the Olympics—it was reward for 50 years of living in the shadow of countries who did not have Canada's history and passion for hockey. In those dry years, no one remembered who came in second.

The Americans would not be an easy team for the Canadians to beat. The U.S. team had improved their play as the tournament pro-gressed and had a high level of confidence after achieving a hard-fought victory against the Russian squad. The Americans had the scoring talents of players such as Brett Hull and Mike Modano and the solid-under-pressure goaltending of Mike Richter.

Even politicians turned out to watch the game. Deputy Prime Minister John Manley represented Canada, while the U.S. brought out Vice-President Dick Cheney to watch the two neighbouring countries do battle on the ice.

After the opening-game ceremonies, the crowd woke up as the teams circled in their own zone ready to take the first face-off of the game. While U.S. fans were clearly in the majority, the Canadian supporters were conspicuous. Team Canada jerseys and Canadian flags dotted the arena.

The Americans came out of the gate first, springing several two-on-one breaks into the Canadian zone. They got a goal by forward Tony Amonte at 8:49 of the first period, when goaltender Martin Brodeur was caught off guard. This was the first time in the tournament that the opposing team had been the first to score, but the Canadian team did not crumble.

They got their confidence back on one of the prettiest goals of the tournament. Controlling the puck through the neutral zone, defenceman Chris Pronger, with Mario Lemieux and Paul Kariya, moved into the U.S. defensive zone where two defencemen waited. The Mario Lemieux of the 1980s came back for a brief moment of magic when he avoided the Pronger pass by letting it glide between his legs, faking out the defencemen and the goaltender who had thought Lemieux was going to take a shot. Instead Lemieux had let it go to Kariya who scored with an easy snapshot into the open net. This highlight-reel goal energized the Canadians who, led by Joe Sakic, took control of the game from that moment on.

Sakic was the all-around best player with the perfect mix of defensive strategy and offensive intelligence. He set up Jerome Iginla with a goal-mouth pass that put Canada up 2–1 going into the second period. Brian Rafalski tied the game on a power-play goal with less than five minutes remaining in the second period and brought the quiet American fans back to life. But the celebrations stopped short when Sakic put the Canadians back on top with a power-play goal of his own with just 1:20 remaining in the period. Canada went into the dressing room for the second intermission, confident they could put the game away in the third.

The third period was the most intense of the match. The Americans sought to get a crucial goal or two. The Canadians held firm, and Martin Brodeur kept his team alive with spectacular saves. The crowd noise swelled to a deafening roar that made the 8250 fans seem more like 18,000. Those watching in the arena were on the edge of their seats, including Canadian team manager Wayne Gretzky, who jumped and gasped like every Canadian fan in the building and at home watching the game.

Worries of a U.S. comeback were wiped aside with Canada's fourth goal. Steve Yzerman, who had just returned to the ice after serving two tense minutes in the penalty box for tripping, picked up the puck and passed it to Iginla. Iginla blasted a shot at the top corner that Richter stopped with his glove, but the puck fell to the ice and rolled over the goal line to put Canada up 4–2 with just four minutes remaining in the third period. Joe Sakic sealed the deal just two minutes later with a breakaway goal. As the buzzer sounded to end the game, goaltender Martin Brodeur leaped into the air and was quickly surrounded by his teammates. Fifty years to the day, Canada was once again at the top.

"We had a great game plan in place and played it to a 'T,'" said Chris Pronger in a Canadian Press interview after the game. "And Marty Brodeur made some great stops towards the end to preserve the victory."

The significance of the win could be seen on the face of each player when a gold medal was placed around his neck. As the Canadian anthem played, many had tears of joy in their eyes for what they had just accomplished.

"It's unbelievable," said Pronger. "It's something you'll always be able to cherish, especially having it here in North America."

Only after the tournament did everyone find out that the Olympic Games icemaker, a Canadian, had buried a Canadian "loonie" for good luck under centre ice.

Hockey fans across Canada celebrated the gold medal win, knowing it wasn't an easy road to victory. Next stop, Olympic Winter Games 2006?

Canadian Women Keep on Winning

At the same time that Canada watched its men's team win gold at the 2002 Winter Olympic Games, another Canadian hockey team was making Olympic history of its own at Salt Lake City.

In the early 1990s, Canadian women's hockey existed in the shadow of the more popular and better-funded men's national hockey program. The first international women's hockey tournament was barely mentioned in the media. The women's neon pink uniforms did not help in promoting the new venture in sport. Even though Canadian women won the first World Championship, winning all five of their games and scoring 61 goals, it was men's teams that got the attention.

Regardless of the lack of attention, the Canadian women's team dominated the international scene, winning the world championships in 1992, 1994 and 1997. After the '97 championship win, the public began to come around, and the media jumped on the rivalry that was developing between Canada and the U.S. At the beginning of 1997, the U.S. women's team could not match the skill of the Canadians. Over the year, they worked hard and developed a solid core of players, led by Cammi Granato, that was able to challenge the Canadian team and provide exciting hockey for the fans.

That was the situation as women's hockey was set to be played at the Olympics for the first time in the 1998 Winter Olympics in Nagano, Japan. Now that national pride was on the table, Canadian women hockey players had special training regimens, coaches and other perks the men's teams had long enjoyed.

Canada and the U.S. easily made their way through the other countries at the 1998 Olympics and found themselves face to face in the gold-medal game. The United States wanted revenge for their razor-thin defeat at the 1997 World Championships, which they had lost in overtime on a goal from Canadian Nancy Drolet.

The Canadian team had everything to lose in this game. They had held the world championship title since international women's hockey began. They wanted to prove they were the best in the first Olympic women's hockey game.

Unfortunately, they didn't play like the team that had won the other tournaments. The gold-medal game began with the United States taking control immediately, connecting most of their passes and getting a flurry of shots off at over-worked Canadian goaltender Manon Rheaume. Canada played like a team of individuals and not the effective unit that they had once been. In the final minutes of the third period, the U.S. was leading 2–1. Canada pulled their goaltender for an extra attacker hoping to tie the game and send it into overtime. But Canada could not keep control of the puck, and the Americans scored an empty-net goal for a 3–1 victory, winning the first gold medal for Olympic women's hockey. The emotion of the moment overcame the Canadian team, who felt the disappointment of their country on their shoulders.

"At first, you feel disbelief," said Canadian team captain Stacy Wilson after the gold-medal loss. "You have a dream for so many years and all of a sudden it's over. Then, the thoughts go through your head of your family and friends all over Canada…and thoughts lead to feelings. You see the medal and its silver—feelings kick in pretty quick."

"They were extremely hungry," Canadian defender Judy Diduck said. "We've been on top so long; we won all the major tournaments. They were determined to knock us off."

Team Canada regained some confidence with a World Championship win in 1999 and was ready to meet the United States for a rematch at the 2002 Winter Olympic Games in Salt Lake City. The Canadian team went into the games as the favourites to win the silver and were not expected to provide a challenge to the U.S. team who had won eight games in a row against the Canadian squad during the season leading up to the Olympics.

Assistant captain and arguably the heart of the Canadian team, Hayley Wickenheiser, said before the tournament started, "I've never lost eight games in a row in my entire hockey career. This is tough, but it's going to make Salt Lake City that much better. We have a lot to prove, and we have nothing to lose now."

The Canadian squad played their system in the first few games and dominated the competition, beating Kazakhstan 7–0, Russia 7–0 and Sweden 11–0. Canadian goaltender Kim St-Pierre made key saves, while her teammates ran away with the game. Canada was on a high. Canadian jerseys popped up all over the arena as the tournament went on. The chants of "Go, Canada, Go!" got louder and louder.

The first real challenge of the tournament for the Canadian women came when they faced off against a much-improved Finnish team. In the first period, the game went according to plan for the Canadians with Canada potting 2 goals and ending the period ahead 2–1 after a late Finnish goal. Canada made 22 shots on the opposing goal in the second period but could not again get the puck behind tiny Finnish goaltender Tuula Puputti. By the end of the second period, Finland had scored two more goals and was poised to upset the Canadians.

Despite the sobering score, the Canadian players did not change their game plan when the third period got underway. Their continuing hard offence eventually paid off. The Finnish goaltender did her best to keep the Canadians at bay but could not stop all the shots. Just three minutes into the third period Hayley Wickenheiser and Jayna Hefford scored two nice breakaway goals just six seconds apart. After that, the Finnish team could not hold the Canadians. Canada ended the game with a 7–3 victory and a path to the gold-medal game against their rivals, the United States. Canada went into the gold-medal game feeling confident they could win.

"Our team is good enough to win gold," said Canadian defenceman Geraldine Heaney in a Canadian Press interview after the Canada-Finland game. "We came here for a gold medal and nothing else. It comes down to one game, and anything can happen."

The Americans were the odds-on favourites having been undefeated in the previous 35 games. The hometown U.S. crowd welcomed their team with a roof-raising cheer as the teams hit the ice for the pre-game skate. Canadian fans supporting their country's team were a sea of red and white. Wayne Gretzky showed up with a large contingent from the Canadian men's squad to cheer on their female counterparts. The noise of the crowd was deafening when the American referee dropped the puck to start the game.

The Americans seemed nervous in the first few minutes of the game. Canada quickly capitalized with a goal by left wing Caroline Ouellette at just 1:45 in the game. As the first period came to a close, Canada knew that they had the Americans scrambling. The Canadian team was controlling the flow of the game despite four questionable penalties given to the Canadians by American referee Stacey Livingston.

More penalties against Canada came at the start of the second period, and the Americans overcame the goaltending of Kim St-Pierre on a power-play goal by Katie King. Just a few minutes later, Canada restored its lead on a goal by Hayley Wickenheiser. The Canadians were winning the battle on the ice and also in the stands, as chants of "Go, Canada, Go!" got louder. The chant grew louder after a dramatic goal from Canada's Jayna Hefford in the final seconds of the second period.

After a breakdown in the neutral zone by the American defence, Hefford picked up a loose puck and out-skated a defenceman for a breakaway on U.S. goaltender Sara DeCosta. As Hefford broke in over the American blue line with the defenceman on her tail, she fumbled with the puck but somehow managed to poke the puck over the sprawled-out goaltender with one second remaining on the clock. It was not the prettiest of breakaway goals, but Canada now had a 2-goal cushion going into the third period.

The U.S. came within 1 goal of Canada's score but couldn't get any closer against the goaltending of Kim St-Pierre. As the seconds peeled off the clock, the Canadians knew they would be wearing the Olympic Gold around their necks this time.

"We stayed calm. We could see the fear in their eyes," said a confident Wickenheiser after the game.

In the dying seconds of the game, the Canadian national anthem could be heard throughout the arena in a show of support for the team that no one expected would beat the Americans. When the clock ran out, the Canadian bench cleared, and the team surrounded their star goaltender in celebration.

This time it was Canada's turn to stand proudly with the gold medals around their necks and listen to their anthem. They had earned the victory. They had earned the moment in the spotlight.

Chapter Four

The Weird, Wild and Weary Moments in Hockey

Lord Stanley's Cup is Born

Ever since Canada's Governor General Lord Stanley purchased the Dominion Hockey Challenge Cup for about $50 in 1892, hockey players from every country have made holding that trophy their lifelong goal.

Although Lord Stanley never played the game, his sons were involved in the formation of an Ottawa team called the Rideau Rebels. It was Lord Stanley's idea to purchase a trophy that teams in the Dominion of Canada would play to win.

Although the original Cup was only 18 centimetres high, with it Lord Stanley started one of the greatest traditions in sports. Its name, The Dominion of Hockey Challenge Cup, was shortened to the Stanley Cup after Montréal's AAA team won it for the first time in 1893.

Ironically the namesake of the Cup never saw it awarded. He was recalled to duties in England where he passed away in 1908. Yet his legacy lives on every year when National Hockey League champions hoist the trophy above their heads.

The Death of Howie Morenz: Hockey Mourns its First Superstar

Howie Morenz was more than just one of the best hockey players ever to set his skates on the ice: he was a legend in his own time. He moved the hearts and imagination of a country that followed his every move. He was hockey's first superstar, and everyone loved to watch Howie Morenz play the game.

His short 1.75-metre height and light 75-kilo weight did not stop him from playing hockey as successfully as those much bigger. He bounced off opposing players as he sped up the ice, arriving alone at the other end with only a poor goaltender left to stop him.

"He's the hardest player in the league to stop," recalled Boston's hard-nosed defenceman Eddie Shore, often the victim of Morenz's end-to-end rushes.

Like many hockey greats, Morenz was an unlikely hero. He was humble about his talents on the ice and private about his life off the ice. When Montréal Canadiens' management first came calling to his hometown of Stratford, Ontario, Morenz refused to join the team because he thought he wasn't good enough.

After seeing the Toronto St. Pat's play, he told his mother, "You don't have to worry about me becoming a professional—those fellows are far too good." Morenz might not have recognized his talent, but hockey scouts knew a superstar when they saw one.

It did not take long for Morenz to make his mark and find a place at the front of the Montréal Canadiens' roster. Teamed up with established star Aurele Joliat for the 1923–24 season, the tandem helped secure the Canadiens their first Stanley Cup in the NHL. Morenz scored 7 goals in the 6 playoff games played by the Canadiens and quickly became the talk of the town.

In the book *Lions in Winter*, Joliat remembered what it was like to play with Morenz in those early days with the Canadiens, "I played with him but not exactly with him, if you get what I mean. I was always in front of him or behind him. I could never stay even with him, that's for sure. J**** C*****, could he go! End-to-end rushes…None of this back-and-forth passing to get there…he went straight from end to end."

Through the cigarette–smoke-filled Montréal Forum, when Morenz began to work his way up the ice, a chant, "Les Canadiens sont la," spread to every person in the building until it reached a fever pitch when Morenz broke into the opponent's zone and scored. As quickly as he moved up the ice, Morenz sped back into his zone to stop any odd-man rushes. Millions of people followed his exploits on the ice and over the airwaves. He became a major draw wherever he went.

As much as Morenz revelled in winning, he detested losing. In a playoff game against Boston, Morenz took the faceoff in overtime against big Cooney Weiland. When the puck was dropped, it took a strange bounce and flew into the air. Morenz and Weiland both swung at the puck, but it was Weiland who connected and scored the winning goal.

Montréal sportswriter Elmer Ferguson remembered later how, at 4:00 the next morning, he answered a knock at his hotel door and found an emotionally beat-up Morenz, his head hanging low. "He was in complete despair. He'd been walking the streets since the game ended, berating himself for Weiland's goal."

It was these moments that made him so well liked among the Canadiens' faithful. Between 1923 and 1933, Morenz led the Canadiens to three Stanley Cups, and he won three Hart Trophies as league MVP and two Art Ross Trophies as top scorer. In the 1930s, after 10 years of battling on the boards for the puck and sprinting up the ice, Morenz began to slow down. His feet weren't moving as fast as they used to; his shots were not as hard; and the goals didn't come as often as they once had. Morenz ended up ninth overall in scoring, and the Canadiens hovered near the bottom of the league.

When boos began to pour down from the stands at the Montréal Forum, Morenz took it to heart. When the Canadiens decided to trade the "Stratford Streak" to the Chicago Blackhawks, Morenz was beside himself with anger at the Canadiens' management. Morenz knew he still had some good years of hockey left in him, and he knew he would prove the naysayers wrong.

Although hockey fans in Chicago knew who Howie Morenz was, they did not have the love affair with him that Montréal had built up over the years. After an unproductive stint in Chicago, Morenz was traded to the Rangers where the same pattern repeated itself. Then he got a call from Cecil Hart who had agreed to coach the Canadiens on the condition that Morenz was brought back to Montréal. At the age of 34, Morenz was back in the city he loved with the team he loved and started to play like the Morenz that had won over the hearts of the Habs' fans. However, his luck drastically changed on the night of January 28, 1937.

That night, the Canadiens took on the Chicago Blackhawks at the Montréal Forum under the watchful eye of a capacity crowd. The mood in the building was upbeat. The Canadiens were at the top of their division, and Morenz was up to his old tricks again. The mood changed during the first period when Morenz raced into the corner to pick up the puck. His skate got caught in the boards just as Chicago defenceman big Earl Siebert crashed into him from behind. Morenz's body twisted around in the crash. The fans throughout the Forum heard the *crack* from his ankle and leg breaking in several places.

Doctors told Morenz he would never play hockey again. Although he had many visitors to his bed, Morenz sank into depression. His visitors could see the injury was breaking his heart.

After lying in bed for a month, a tired and frustrated Morenz decided he'd had enough hospital rest. On the night of March 8, 1937, still in his plaster cast, he forced himself out of bed, took one step and fell to the floor, dead.

Doctors reported the cause of death as a "cardiac deficiency and acute excitement." His friends and family knew his death was at least partially due to the pain of knowing he would never play hockey again.

"To the hockey palace his fame helped to build and where he knew his greatest triumphs, the body of Howie Morenz was taken today for public services," ran one Montréal newspaper account of his funeral.

On March 11, 1937, 15,000 people jammed the Montréal Forum for the funeral services. Thousands more waited outside for their chance to file past the coffin to pay final respects to the man who had given them so much.

Aurele Joliat, Morenz's long-time friend and linemate, saw Morenz' death as a tragic waste. "Howie loved to play hockey more than anyone ever loved anything, and when he realized that he would never play again...Howie died of a broken heart."

"He was the greatest of all time," remembered coach Dick Irvin, "and the world of hockey will seem bereft without him."

Montréal Rocked by Richard Riot

By the time the 1954–55 NHL season began, Maurice Richard's temper was well known. In fact, players on other teams often tried to exploit his push-button rage. None were more aware of the Rocket's misdeeds than NHL President Clarence Campbell. Campbell and the Rocket had butted heads on several issues. The mistrust and dislike between them became the catalyst for the Richard Riots of March 1955.

In December 1954, Richard was forced to apologize to President Campbell for a series of articles that he had ghostwritten. The articles, published in a French-language paper, harshly criticized Campbell both personally and professionally. In the articles, Richard called Campbell the league's "Dictator" and charged him with openly cheering other teams when they scored against the predominantly French-Canadian Montréal Canadiens. Richard even goaded Campbell into taking action against him, saying, "If Mr. Campbell wants to throw me out of the league for daring to criticize him, let him do it." The incident cost Richard $1000 and a public apology but earned him a place in the hearts of French-Canadian fans. They saw Richard as an "everyman" figure fighting against the elitist English establishment. It didn't hurt that he could score a goal like no one else.

Penalties were not enough to deter the Rocket. He continued to rack up fines for getting under Clarence Campbell's skin.

Another episode of the drama took place during a game against long-time rivals and Campbell favourites, the Toronto Maple Leafs. The clock was winding down on an exciting but relatively non-violent game between the Leafs and the Canadiens. With just a few minutes remaining, all hell broke loose. Richard became involved in a scuffle with Leafs forward Bob Bailey. Instead of swinging, Bailey tried to gouge out Richard's eyes. Richard lost his temper and went berserk. He knocked out two of Bailey's teeth.

Referee Red Storey remembered the incident in Dick Irvin's book *The Habs*. "Every time we'd get the Rocket straightened out, he'd go over to the bench and Dick [Irvin Sr.] would give him another stick. When we saw the replay, he'd had five different sticks before it was over. He wasn't hunting for trouble any night. But I'll tell you, when trouble started, he finished it."

Richard was fined $250 for the incident. No matter how many fines he threw at Richard, Campbell knew it would not stop him from participating in another incident.

"For every $250 I fined him, Québec businessmen would send him $1000," said Campbell, knowing Richard's popularity in Québec. "Richard could do no wrong in Québec. I was always the villain."

The events leading to the riots continued during a game between the Canadiens and the Boston Bruins on March 13, 1955. With only four games remaining in the regular season, the Canadiens wanted to end their rivalry with the Bruins on a high note, but Boston had a 4–2 lead late in the third period. At one point in the game, Boston defenceman Hal Laycoe and Richard met on the ice for one of the most infamous fights in hockey.

"On this particular night, the Bruins were really up for us. They laid on the lumber at every opportunity, and by the time the game had reached the end of the first period, we were a very bruised bunch of men," noted Richard, as he looked back on the Laycoe incident.

The incident happened when Laycoe and Richard both rushed into a corner after the puck and collided in a mess of arms and sticks. Richard got the worst of the hit. As he fell to the ice, his stick caught Laycoe on the head, opening up a gash that poured blood. Laycoe, furious from the injury, swung his stick at Richard several times, catching him on the side of the head and opening a "bleeder" that trickled down Richard's face into his eyes. When Richard saw the blood, he lost his cool. His eyes changed—he became a man on a mission, and Laycoe was the target. The two started swinging their sticks: sometimes aiming at shoulders, sometimes at heads. Sometimes they swung with both hands.

Hoping to stop the fight before anyone was seriously hurt, linesman Cliff Thompson jumped in and tried to break it up. When Thompson grabbed Richard to hold him back from Laycoe, Richard broke free and lunged at the Bruin defenceman several times. Fed up with Thompson's intervention, Richard warned Thompson not to grab him from behind again. Thompson, however, did so and pinned Richard down on the ice. This sent Richard into a fury. Seeing his teammate pinned by the linesman, Canadiens defenceman Doug Harvey knocked Thompson off the enraged Richard. Richard jumped up and punched the linesman twice in the face. Richard felt the punch was deserved—after all, he had warned Thompson.

"He wouldn't listen. That's why I hit him," said Richard.

What is often omitted from the story is that Thompson, at one time, had been a defenceman for the Boston Bruins. Whether this was a factor in the melee is not known, but it is interesting to note that Thompson did not officiate another game in the NHL. For his actions, Richard was thrown out of the game. He knew he would be having another meeting with Campbell because of this incident.

On the train ride back to Montréal, the team was ominously silent. Richard sat quietly staring out the window feeling that his actions were justified, but he expected Campbell's reaction would not help his team. Team owners across the League condemned Richard as a loose cannon who should be dealt with harshly. It was left to NHL President Clarence Campbell to decide how Richard should be punished.

French media in Montréal were in an uproar over having the fate of their hero in the hands of Campbell, who was known for his personal dislike of Richard, the Canadiens and French Canadians in general. The situation was a focus of the restlessness that had been building among French Canadians for some time. The French majority in Québec was increasingly angered by the social and wage discrepancies that existed between it and the Anglophone minority in that province. Montréal had seen a number of demonstrations by the French, and the Richard affair seemed ready to light the fuse on the tense situation.

After some deliberation, Campbell came down with the verdict in an official 18-paragraph document that spelled out the reasons for the course of action he had chosen. All the Montréal fans needed to read was the final sentence: "Richard will be suspended from all games, both league and playoff, for the balance of the current season."

Front-page headlines in the French Montréal papers echoed the sentiment prevalent in the city:

La Presse: "Too Harsh a Penalty: Mayor Drapeau hoping for a review of sentence."

Montréal-Matin: "Victim of yet another injustice, the worst ever, Maurice Richard will play no more this season."

At Richard's home, phone calls of support came in from people he knew and many he didn't.

"Rocket! We're going to get even with Campbell. There's going to be a lot of trouble at the Forum tonight."

"It's an injustice! Campbell will get what is coming to him!"

Campbell was getting phone calls at his home of a less supportive nature. Despite death threats, Campbell was not deterred from enforcing his decision on Richard's suspension. He even announced that he would appear at the next Canadiens' game at the Forum.

Campbell said defiantly, "It is my right and my duty to be present at the game both as a citizen and as president of the league, and if the mayor or Forum authorities had an apprehension they would not be able to deal with and had requested me to absent myself, I would gladly comply with their request."

On the evening of March 17, 1955, the Canadiens were taking on their long-time rivals the Detroit Red Wings, who were two points behind in the overall standings. Among the 16,000 fans at the Forum was a nervous but defiant Clarence Campbell. Outside, angry fans gathered in increasing numbers, chanting slogans supporting Richard and denouncing Campbell: "Vive Richard!"; "Campbell Drop Dead!"; "Richard, the Persecuted!"

With the game already underway, Campbell took his seat to a chorus of boos and had to dodge occasional tomatoes thrown at him. As the game proceeded, the crowd focused less on what was happening on the ice and more on the league president sitting in the stands. A young man wearing a leather jacket approached Campbell near the end of the first period under the pretence of shaking the president's hand but instead punched him several times before police intervened. Then a tear gas bomb exploded sending a cloud of acrid smoke through the Forum. Patrons rushed for the exits.

The 250 police officers on site were not able to control the chaos, as the 10,000 irate fans exited the building and joined the thousands of angry protesters outside the Forum. The excitement carried outside sparked the angry crowd, turning it into a mob. The mob moved down St-Catherine Street, smashing windows, setting fires and overturning cars. By the time the violence died down at 3:00 AM, the west end of downtown Montréal had been laid to waste.

Richard was appalled by the violence. Yet, he felt the affair would not have reached the peak it did had Campbell not appeared at the Forum.

"What Campbell did was no more sensible than waving a red flag in front of an angry bull," said Richard.

Urged on by Frank Selke, the general manager of the Montréal Canadiens, Richard spoke on the local radio in both languages the morning after the riot and appealed for calm. "I will take my punishment," he said, "and come back next year."

That morning, citizens of Montréal were ashamed of what they had done to their city in the name of their hero who did not condone such actions. Adding further insult, the Detroit Red Wings beat the Canadiens in the Stanley Cup finals that year.

With Maurice back the following year, the Canadiens finished on top of the league and won the first of what would be five straight Stanley Cups. *L'Affair Richard*, as it is called in French, secured Maurice Richard's status as a cultural icon in Québec and a legend in hockey that has yet to see his equal.

The Highs and Lows of Terry Sawchuk

Night after night it is the goaltender's job to stand at solitary attention waiting for the opposing team to rush up the ice to hack, slash and slap the puck into the net. Goaltenders are saddled with the responsibility of being the last line between a team's victory and its defeat. They are the most solitary players on the ice. They have only themselves to blame for their triumphs and defeats— they either stop the puck or they don't, plain and simple. It takes a special kind of person to stand in front of a frozen rubber disc travelling at 160 kilometres per hour with nothing but a few inches of padding and without a mask for face protection. No other hockey player mirrored the requirements of his position better than Sawchuk.

Sawchuk got his first taste of goaltending with his Bantam A team in his hometown of Winnipeg, when the team's goalie quit. The coach decided to try Sawchuk in the net because his brother, who had died at 17 of a heart condition, had been an excellent goaltender. Terry wore his dead brother's pads when he played his first game in net. From then on, he never left the position he would revolutionize. After a brilliant minor-league career, Sawchuk made his way into the NHL with the Detroit Red Wings in the 1949–50 season. He impressed Detroit general manager Jack Adams enough for Adams to cast aside veteran goalie Harry Lumley and sign up Sawchuk.

During his first full season with the Red Wings, Sawchuk established himself as the team's number-one goaltender, playing all 70 games, winning the Calder Trophy as the top rookie in the league and being named to the first of many all-star games. He finished the season with a goals-against average of 1.90 and had 12 shutouts to his credit.

Despite his success, Sawchuk took each win and loss personally. This emotional intensity was reflected in the way he dealt with his teammates.

"[Sawchuk is] a strange bird," a fellow Red Wings teammate once said of him. "You can be joking with him one minute in the dressing room, and then you'll see him walking down the street later, and he'll walk right by you."

Sawchuk came into his own during the Red Wings' stellar 1951–52 season, when they finished first in the standings and were the favourites to win the Stanley Cup. Led by Sawchuk and "The Production Line," a forward line composed of Gordie Howe, Ted Lindsay and Sid Abel, the Wings easily defeated the Toronto Maple Leafs in the first round of the playoffs and then waited while the Canadiens battled out a long seven-game series against the Boston Bruins.

Both the Canadiens and the Red Wings played an open style of hockey that focused on deadly accurate offensive talents. Sawchuk's job was not an easy one.

The Canadiens had a talented offense led by Maurice "the Rocket" Richard whose moves were hard to predict. Richard could score on a goaltender in a hundred different ways, and he never chose the same way twice. The Canadiens, however, did not have much energy left after the long series against the Bruins and had a difficult time overcoming Sawchuk's goaltending. They scored only two goals in the first two games of the series. In the next two games, in Detroit, Sawchuk had two shutouts and led his team to the Stanley Cup. Sawchuk had won eight straight games, allowing only five goals and had a record playoff goals-against average of 0.62 that to this day hasn't been beaten.

Part mental and part physical, Sawchuk's style was totally natural. He had a wide body frame that covered most of the net leaving only small openings; he had lighting-quick reflexes that compensated for the spaces left open. Some of his success was due to the fact that the players he faced had never seen a style like his before. Sawchuk brought an innovation to goaltending. In an era when most goaltenders practiced an upright stance, Sawchuk crouched low to the ground. He was thus able to see the puck at a better angle, and his arms were cocked at his sides ready to shoot out and grab a blistering slapshot. The stance also enabled him to drop to the ice to stop low shots quicker than stand-up goaltenders, and it increased his ability to move laterally and to use his leg or glove for one of his explosive saves.

In the book *Without Fear*, goaltending legend Johnny Bower commented on Sawchuk's style:

Terry Sawchuk is the greatest goaltender ever. He was the kind of player who [only] went through the motions in practice and warm-up but, come game time, there was none better. One of Terry's strengths was his crouch—it was one of the best that I'd ever witnessed. He remained square to the shooter as much as possible but cheated on rushes in that he wasn't the quickest goalie to come out and cut down the angle. But his cat-like reflexes were what allowed him to stay a little deeper in the net.

Sawchuk's mental game was one of his biggest assets. He played every game like it was overtime in game seven of the Stanley Cup finals. The intensity made him the successful goaltender he was, but it also brought him pain and anguish. On the ice, Sawchuk was not one to shy away from confronting fans who taunted him. Off the ice he was hard to get along with, losing his temper at the slightest provocation. His intense approach brought him success, but it also brought him pain.

Plagued by injuries, illness, countless operations and stress, Sawchuk often joked that when he wasn't playing hockey, he spent his time in the hospital. His weight was often a measure of his health, at one point jumping from a low of 74 kilograms to a high of 104 kilograms—very heavy for a man standing only 1.8 metres.

One just has to look at a photo of Sawchuk's face taken for *Life* magazine in 1966 to know the amount of abuse he took tending goal for a living. The photograph shows the amount of scar tissue on his face left from sticks, pucks and fists he had encountered over the course of his career and had repaired with more than 400 stitches.

Yet, despite his injuries and bad luck, Sawchuk was the best in the league. By the end of his fifth season, he had amassed an amazing 57 shutouts. Things went bad for Sawchuk, however, when Red Wings general manager Jack Adams traded Sawchuk and replaced him with Glenn Hall. Hall had played a few games for Detroit when Sawchuk was out of commission and had impressed Adams. Sawchuk was not the only one surprised by the move. The entire league questioned Detroit trading away its star goaltender for an unknown talent.

Sawchuk was not happy to be in Boston. The Bruins were at the bottom of the league and had no hope of getting into the playoffs. For the first time Sawchuk's goals-against average went above 2.00 ending the 1955–56 season at 2.60.

His health also took a turn for the worse. After looking sluggish in several games, he was diagnosed with mononucleosis. After a brief rest at home, Sawchuk returned to the ice, but he wasn't the same goaltender he'd been just a year before. Still, he was good enough that Boston, with Sawchuk in net, rose in the overall standings.

By January, Sawchuk had had enough of the stress and doubts about his health. He announced he was retiring from hockey. He jumped on a train back to his home in Detroit and never returned to Boston.

In Detroit, his physician announced, "Mr. Sawchuk is on the verge of a complete nervous breakdown." Sawchuk took the rest of the season off to spend time with his family and get away from the pressures of professional hockey.

People who knew Sawchuk were not surprised when they saw him at the Detroit training camp that fall preparing himself for the start of the 1957–58 season. Everyone who knew Sawchuk understood that hockey was his life, and that until he could not put on a pair of skates, nothing would keep him from the game he loved.

As the years flew by, the legend of Terry Sawchuk got bigger and so did the problems following him. He was always insecure about his performance. Teammates never knew whether Sawchuk was in a good mood or not.

"He liked to present himself as this moody, aloof person, because then people would leave him alone," said long-time friend and Red Wings teammate Marcel Pronovost in the book *Without Fear*. "One time a young boy got hit with a puck during a game. They brought him into the dressing room afterward, and Terry got his stick signed by all the players and gave it to the boy. Then he turned to me and said, 'If you tell the press about this, I'll kill you.' That's the way he was."

Sawchuk admitted to his failings in an interview with *Maclean's* writer Trent Frayne. "The crazy thing is, though, that when I'm actually on the ice I don't worry at all— it's only before the game or between periods that I really brood."

Although Sawchuk was happy to be back with the Detroit team, it was not winning at the rate it had been two years earlier. Detroit was fighting to stay out of the bottom of the league. Still, Sawchuk was producing good results. In the 1963–64 season at the age of 35, he recorded his 95th shutout, surpassing legendary Montréal Canadiens goaltender George Hainsworth's career record of 94. Record aside, Sawchuk's talent between the pipes was diminishing as time and injuries caught up with him.

The NHL changed during the 1960s. Hockey became more of a science as players like Bobby Hull and Bobby Orr opened up the game. Goaltenders had their first introduction to curved sticks. Goaltenders could no longer anticipate where a shot would go as pucks, visibly arcing in the air, were sent off curved sticks in any direction. Goaltenders became more vulnerable. An old stalwart like Sawchuk no longer produced the same numbers he had early in his career.

Sawchuk was shipped off to the Toronto Maple Leafs where he joined another aging veteran goaltender by the name of Johnny Bower. Sawchuk's old moody ways continued with his new team. Although good friends, the two goaltenders had different approaches to the game. Whereas Bower was one of the hardest-working players on the team and often stayed late at practices, Sawchuk put little effort into training for games to the dismay of coaches and management.

Toronto Coach Punch Imlach asked Sawchuk why he didn't put any effort into stopping the puck during the practices, to which Sawchuk replied, "I figure I only have so many saves left in me, and I want to save them for the games." At 37 years old, Sawchuk didn't have many left.

In the 1966–67 season, Sawchuk achieved the 100th shutout game in his career. He and Bower led the Maple Leafs in a stellar performance to take the Stanley Cup. It was one of Sawchuk's last moments of glory. He spent one season in Los Angeles after the expansion draft and ended his career with the New York Rangers having achieved a shutout total of 103.

"One hundred and three shutouts—that's incredible," said goaltender Chris Osgood. "That's like a player scoring 1000 goals."

Unfortunately, Sawchuk's career did not end with the big ceremony he deserved. Instead of a celebration of a career of outstanding highlights, it ended with a sombre memorial remembering a life taken too soon.

After the Rangers were eliminated from the 1970 playoffs, Sawchuk, then 40 years old, was involved in a scuffle with teammate Ron Stewart over who would clean the home they shared. While it remains unclear what happened in the altercation, apparently Sawchuk fell and sustained internal injuries. He was rushed to the hospital. The injuries would have meant only a routine hospital visit for a healthy person but for the weather-worn goaltender plagued by injuries, ill health and hard drinking, it meant several major operations and a lengthy stay. On May 31, 1970, Sawchuk died in his sleep from a blood clot in his lungs.

"The way he lived his life," said friend Marcel Pronovost, "it seemed like he was asking for it."

Regardless of how his life ended, Terry Sawchuk is remembered as one of the greatest goaltenders to stand on the ice.

The Trade: The Great One Goes to Los Angeles

In 1988, Wayne Gretzky, Edmonton's adopted son, had just won the city its fourth Stanley Cup. He was riding a wave of support from Oilers fans and people across Canada. In his eight years since joining the National Hockey League, Gretzky had broken several records, won Canada glory at the '87 Canada Cup and made the Edmonton Oilers the best team in the NHL. Gretzky was Canada's proud little secret, and nobody wanted to share.

Rumours had been flying around for months that the Edmonton Oilers were on the verge of a major player deal involving Gretzky. Most people did not pay attention to rumours during the hockey off-season because each summer rumours abound, usually groundless, about who will be traded. So people were caught off guard when a press conference was called by the Oilers' management on August 9, 1988, to announce a trade.

The pressroom was quiet while Oilers' management walked in and took their seats. Looking rather sedate, Edmonton Oilers' owner Peter Pocklington shifted in his seat, shuffled a few papers in front of him and took a deep breath before making his shattering announcement.

"Gretzky has been traded to the Los Angeles Kings," said Pocklington, while flashes from cameras illuminated the room.

The media had not been aware that Pocklington and charismatic Kings' owner Bruce McNall had signed a deal two weeks earlier. The press conference had been postponed for two weeks, because the Oilers' season-ticket drive was on, and the news of its star player being traded would have hurt sales. Gretzky had been packaged with enforcer Marty McSorley and Mike Krushelnyski and traded for Jimmy Carson and Martin Gelinas. In addition, Oilers' management also were given several first-round draft picks in 1989, 1991 (used to acquire Martin Rucinsky) and 1993 (used to acquire Nick Stajduhar) and $15 million in cash.

After Peter Pocklington finished reading from the papers in front of him, it was time for Gretzky to approach the microphone. There were no signs of happiness in Gretzky's face. He took a couple of breaths before confirming the news that nobody wanted to hear.

"For the benefit of Wayne Gretzky, my new wife and our expected child in the new year, it would be for the benefit of everyone involved to let me play for the Los Angeles Kings," said Gretzky, pausing to take a breath. "I promised Mess [Mark Messier] I wouldn't do this," he said, wiping tears from his eyes.

Edmonton and Canada were in collective shock. The boy from Brantford, Ontario, whom the country had watched grow into one of the greatest hockey players had been handed over without a fight to a U.S. team. The newspapers the next day echoed the feelings of sadness and betrayal that ran through Edmonton as people downed the news along with their morning cup of coffee.

"The emotions we're dealing with here are not unlike those of a death in the family. A death not by natural causes," wrote *Edmonton Sun* journalist Terry Jones.

Immediately people began looking for someone to blame, and their eyes fell on much-maligned owner Peter Pocklington. Although at the press conference Gretzky said the decision to go to Los Angeles was his own, speculation persisted that Pocklington had forced him out. There were rumours that Pocklington's other business ventures were in disarray and that the large cash payment included in the Gretzky trade was welcome to the cash-strapped owner. As rumours surfaced over the next few days, Pocklington's tone changed as attacks came at him from all sides.

Pocklington responded with harsh criticism. "If they think their king walked the streets of Edmonton without having a thought of moving, they are under a great delusion. He's a great actor. I thought he pulled it off beautifully when he showed how upset he was, but he wants a big dream," said Pocklington in a *Los Angeles Times* interview.

Gretzky later put the verbal jousting to a halt when he confessed he had asked for the trade to the Los Angeles Kings, although he said he had done so only after exhausting his negotiations with Oilers' management.

"I would've liked to finish my career in Edmonton…I offered to sign an eight-year contract. All they had to do was agree to a no-trade clause. They wouldn't do it," revealed Gretzky.

When all was said and done, Canada's greatest hockey ambassador went south to the United States. A hockey player to whom a country attached so much pride and passion had become a commodity in the business of the National Hockey League. Leaving aside the new players the Oilers picked up, the future seemed bleak for Canadian hockey. Canada had lost its hockey hero.

In contrast to the sadness caused by the announcement in Edmonton, things looked brighter on the other end of the trade. The welcoming party at the Kings' headquarters was a festive affair. Gretzky was all smiles when Bruce McNall handed him his new Los Angeles Kings jersey and officially welcomed him to the organization.

The Gretzky trade was more than just a transfer of a player from one team to another. His arrival in L.A. brought renewed interest to the game of hockey there. A team that had been struggling in points and public support was brought to the forefront of the media's attention. He was a star in a town that worshipped stars.

After the transfer, record numbers of people came out to watch hockey in Los Angeles. At the start of the previous season, only 4500 season tickets had been sold for the Kings' home games. By the night of Gretzky's first home game with the Kings in 1988, 13,000 season tickets had been sold. Tickets for that game were hard to come by.

The Kings' points total went up by 23 that season. The players that flanked Gretzky on the left and right wings had banner years under the Great One's tutelage. Linemate Bernie Nicholls had previously been a pretty decent goal scorer, averaging about 34 goals per season. With Gretzky as his linemate, Nicholls scored a remarkable 70 goals that season.

The Gretzky effect could be felt everywhere in the southern states. Hockey got more television airtime. Leagues sprouted up in the United States. The viability of southern franchises grew, shown by the additions of teams like the Anaheim Mighty Ducks, the Dallas Stars and the San Jose Sharks.

Speculation may continue and blame passed back and forth, but no one can argue that Gretzky did not have a positive effect on the sport of hockey.

"It's the hardest thing I've ever been through. I don't think there's an August 9 where I haven't thought about it," said Gretzky.

Playing Out in the Cold:
Oilers versus Canadiens

Watching hockey outdoors is something that most Canadians have done at least once in their lives, so when the NHL organized an outdoors game for the first time in 90 years, it was a big deal. Dubbed the Heritage Classic, former and current players of the Edmonton Oilers and the Montréal Canadiens played a double header in Edmonton on November 22, 2003, as temperatures hovered around –19°C.

A crowd of 57,167 freezing hockey fans eagerly watched oldtimers, like Bill Ranford, Kevin Lowe, Bobby Smith and Guy Lafleur, perform on the ice for the first time in years. In the first game, the Habs' oldtimers could not match the youth and speed of the Oilers' oldtimers and lost 2–0. Then the 2003 Montréal Canadiens team won the official NHL regular-season game 4–3 over the 2003 Oilers team.

Despite the cold, the two-game event was a complete success with fans. The players said they loved the outdoor game that reminded them of their early years at the local neighbourhood rinks.

NOTES ON SOURCES

Benedict, Michael and D'Arcy Jenish, eds. *Canada On Ice: 50 Years of Great Hockey.* Toronto: Viking Press, 1998.

Diamond, Dan, ed. *Total Hockey.* New York: Total Sports Publishing, 1998.

Dryden, Steve. *The Magic, the Legend, the Numbers: Total Gretzky.* Toronto: McClelland & Stewart Inc., 1999.

Fischler, Stan. *Golden Ice: The Greatest Teams in Hockey History.* Montréal: McGraw-Hill, 1990.

Greig, Murray. *The Biggest Deals in Hockey History.* Toronto: Prentice Hall, 2000.

Irvin, Dick. *The Habs: An Oral History of the Montréal Canadiens 1940–1980.* Toronto: McClelland & Stewart, 1991.

Kendall, Brian. *100 Great Moments in Hockey.* Toronto: Viking, 1994.

MacFarlane, Brian. *The Bruins.* Toronto: Stoddart Press, 1999.

Macskimming, Roy. *Cold War: The Amazing Canada-Soviet Hockey Series of 1972.* Toronto: Greystone Books, 1996.

McDonell, Chris. *For the Love of Hockey: Hockey Stars' Personal Stories.* Richmond Hill: Firefly Books, 2001.

O'Brien, Andy. *The Jacques Plante Story*. Montréal: McGraw-Hill Ryerson Ltd, 1972.

Podnieks, Andrew. *Hockey's Greatest Teams: Teams, Players and Plays that Changed the Game*. Toronto: Penguin Studio, 2000.

Proctor, Stephen, ed. *Canada Gold: Canadian Men & Women Hockey Champions*. Toronto: Winding Stair Press, 2002.

Scanlan, Wayne. "Silver lining tough to find," *The Ottawa Citizen*, February 18, 1998.

Sullivan, Jack. "3-3 Tie Gives Mercurys Olympic Hockey Crown," *Edmonton Journal*, February 25, 1952.

Turowetz, Allan and Chrys Goyens. *Lions In Winter*. Scarborough: Prentice Hall, 1986.